Praise for La

"In her perky, no-nonsense dating manual, Debra Kunz brings her business savvy to the marketplace of romance and teaches women how to date smart and make relationship choices that *really* work."

    --Dr. Alexander Avila, Best Selling Author of *LoveTypes*

"I will give this book to every woman I know who is serious about finding a lasting relationship."

    --Rebecca Forster, USA Today Best Selling Author

"This powerful...book is marketed to women, but men also can benefit from Kunz's insights and obtain increased understanding of the needs of women. I highly recommend this book."

    --Bob Livingstone, LCSW, Author of *Unchain the Pain:*
      How to be Your Own Therapist

"This book is a comprehensive...resource for women entering or re-entering the dating world. Debra has given a straightforward blueprint to navigate this exciting, yet sometimes terrifying, place."

    --Suzy Brown, Founder, Midlife Divorce Recovery, LLC

"Kunz' book is a 'must read' for every dating woman. Its straightforward advice feels like...a wise and trusted friend. This is the stuff your mother never told you and we should all be telling our daughters!"

    --Karen Rowinsky, LSCSW, Therapist in Private Practice

LOVE IS BLIND
ONLY IF YOU ARE

*A Woman's Clear-Headed Guide
to Deliberate Dating*

*Jennifer
Live on purpose*

Debra Kunz

*Love,
Debra Kunz*

BALBOA
PRESS
A DIVISION OF HAY HOUSE

Balboa Press books may be ordered through booksellers or by contacting:

Balboa Press
A Division of Hay House
1663 Liberty Drive
Bloomington, IN 47403
www.balboapress.com
1-(877) 407-4847

Printed in the United States of America

ISBN: 978-1-4525-5597-3 (e)
ISBN: 978-1-4525-5598-0 (sc)
ISBN: 978-1-4525-5599-7 (hc)

Library of Congress Control Number: 2012914386

Balboa Press rev. date: 8/29/2012

For all the women who want something more in their lives and relationships, and especially for those who don't even know it's possible yet.

TABLE OF CONTENTS

ACKNOWLEDGEMENTS

My deepest gratitude to everyone who encouraged and supported me in my journey to write and share *Love is Blind Only if You Are*.

SPECIAL THANKS TO:

Mom – For your belief in me and your author experience.

Barb, Becky, Brenda, Cindy, Diann, and Janet – For your input and candid comments.

Joyce and Stacey – For affirming my vision could become a reality.

Fellow Authors – For understanding the experience of creating my first book.

My Professional Team:

    Robin Blakely – For sharing your writer's wisdom and guidance. www.prtherapy.com

    Caitlin Proctor – For your brilliance creating the cover. www.designcatstudio.com

    Jenny Jensen – For your perspective and editing. www.e-bookeditor.com

    Balboa Press, a division of Hay House Publishing

INTRODUCTION

We love romantic movies where the guy gets the girl and before the credits roll, they're headed blissfully down the aisle. That might be a great wedding event, but is it a relationship? Sometimes the heroine is swept off her feet by a real sleazeball who doesn't deserve to be on the same planet with her. This got me thinking:

- ‣ Why do women make life-long relationship decisions based on what it takes to *get or keep him* instead of what it takes for him to *deserve us?*

- ‣ Why do we run our love lives on default, going through the dating motions until one of the men we meet decides to stay around awhile instead of *choosing* who we *want* to have around?

The default setting is no way to create a joyful, fulfilling life with the love and devotion you seek.

One of the best things I ever did for my love life was to engage my business sense and figure out some dating standards. In business, I begin with "What are we trying to accomplish?" The question creates a common direction and defines the criteria for what you want. Making well thought-out compromises along the way is part of the process. We're being *deliberate*, not making decisions by *default.*

So I ask you - why aren't we using our heads — our *deliberate* self — when it comes to love? Your heart must be part of the process, though it shouldn't be the only factor in choosing who gets a chance. Time and time again, I see women make the same mistakes I have and ignore the <u>B</u>ad <u>A</u>ss <u>T</u>rouble Signs (B.A.T.) when it comes to dating and relationships. It means you settle for what you find, instead of what you want, and compromise yourself in the process... all under the mask of *love*. I learned these lessons the slow, painful way, and sometimes it took more than once, so my intention is to shorten your learning curve.

- It's about choosing not settling.

- Knowing yourself first, before you decide who he should be.

- Having the strength to walk away from a man you know isn't right for you. (I prevented two divorces because I let go of men I knew weren't a match before we headed down the aisle.)

Along with my own love lessons, throughout my life I've been honored that people have sought me out for help, perspective and a voice of reason for their life and relationship problems. After much encouragement to share my experience and practical wisdom with women everywhere, I give you **Love is Blind Only if You Are**. Building the courage to make good deliberate decisions with *your head and your heart* is a devoted theme throughout.

May it bring you some insight, support, laughter, and knowledge. Most importantly, may it empower you, your relationships, and your love life.

Date Deliberately,

Debra

CHAPTER 1

That Dating Place — Is he interested? Am I? How do I know?

Time and time again, I get asked this question. "I'm dating again, Deb," she says with an uncertain smile. "And, I met this guy and I've been out with him a few times. How do I know if he's interested?" To which I respond, "Are *you* interested?"

This is usually followed by silence while she's searching for the *right* answer to the question. Like it's a test she doesn't want to flunk. Like we women are trying to fit ourselves into the mold of the man in front of us and we're not sure how to do that. Like I'm going to tell her how to become something she isn't to please a man she doesn't even know if she likes. So, usually her answer goes something like, "Well... maybe." Followed immediately by, "But is he interested in me? How do I know?"

Welcome to *that dating place*. It's the emotional and mental state where women want to date though they aren't sure how to go about it. Most likely, she hasn't considered what she wants out of the process, nor has she thought about what she needs and what she could give him. Or, more importantly, what she *wants* to give him.

How You Got Here

Some women are coming from a position of strength…with real knowledge and a track record from a previous serious relationship. Maybe you chose a divorce and your decision has completely changed the direction of your life. Some women feel fragile because the divorce wasn't your idea, and the circumstances may be fodder for a mini-series. Or, it could be simpler than that – it was a mutual split because the two of you just weren't the right match, or decided you married too young to know any better. Or maybe you're a widow who's endured a loss and aren't sure what to do now. Could be you're a woman in your twenties and want to learn more about dating. Or, you might be any age and wondering why you're still single.

Regardless of how you got to *that dating place*, welcome. I'm glad you're here to learn, grow and make new choices.

Your Dating Age

Some of you might be thinking, "I should know more about this dating stuff by now. I'm an adult woman. I'm smart. I've raised children (or are raising children.) Ran a household. Ran a business. Have grandchildren. Have a career." Well, let me tell you – your *dating age* has nothing to do with the year you were born. Nothing. Nada. In fact, a big assumption in dating is your chronological age must equal some sort of dating wisdom… like you're smarter at this dating stuff given you are now in your thirties, forties, fifties, or sixties. Nothing could be further from the truth. The common themes for women starting to date, whether they are eighteen or eighty, are the same issues, concerns, mistakes and questions.

Relating Age

Perhaps in your business life, you have more relationship maturity. You understand how business "politics" work, and make good choices accordingly. Or, maybe you don't and your *relating age* is the same in your business and personal life. *Relating age* means your knowledge, experience and comfort in building and maintaining relationships of any type. Careful. Don't let your uncertainty about romantic relationships impact your professional ones.

Your *relating age* affects your ability to build relationships of all types though your *dating age* impacts your love life. Regardless of the context of the relationship, relating to people begins with understanding yourself. Yes, understanding what the other person needs and wants is crucial for long-term success in any relationship, however choosing who gets a chance in your romantic life begins with you, not with him.

The best news about your *dating age* is you don't have to wait a year to celebrate a birthday. Your growth and experience advances at your own pace, not according to the calendar.

What You Don't Know

We all want to trust people will be who they say they are. And, when they're not, we're hurt and confused. No one wants to get hurt, personally or professionally, by any version of a B.A.T. (*Bad Ass Trouble* - much more about those men later) nor do we want to make dumb decisions that hurt us. Yet, we do it anyway by repeating patterns and not really valuing ourselves enough to make different choices. Or, we're so clueless and unaware we don't know what we don't know.

We think we know enough about what *he* should be like, yet haven't taken the time to look at ourselves. We spend a lot of time dissecting his characteristics, strengths, shortcomings and what annoys us, yet haven't examined these things in ourselves yet. This tendency is a glaring issue in all relationships - personal, professional, in your marriage, with your kids, your parents, and your neighbors.

Charging ahead as if the problem lays with everyone else is even a classic issue with business leaders; they decide it's their staff or customers or product that's broken and needs to be fixed when they haven't examined their own contribution to the company's problems. Most likely, the real solution involves a strategy to integrate all of these pieces together and work toward a common direction.

Just like in your love life. Success and *creating deliberate change* starts with recognizing everything begins with understanding yourself, what you want, what's important to you and the components that need to be in place to create it. We'll go deeper into those topics throughout the book and help you discover what you don't know.

What You've Always Done

Every woman (and man for that matter), who is starting to date has the same questions, feels the same insecurities, and makes the same clueless mistakes, regardless of how old they are. The good news is our *dating age* makes us all in our twenties! The bad news is many of us aren't. (For those of you who are, thank goodness you're learning early in life and saving yourself some versions of heartache the rest of us have already been through.)

You continue doing what you've always done and wonder why you detest dating, and why you haven't found anyone you want to spend time with. Or, no one you've been out with wants to spend time with you. So you decide it must be you and you're broken. Or, it's all men, and they are the problem. (Has this ever escaped your lips, "All men are jerks!") Am I getting close? In which camp do you find yourself pitching the tent?

I'm guessing one of your answers was, "It depends." You might go on to say, "The last guy was…. Well the one before that was…." Or, "I haven't been out with anyone yet 'cause I'm too scared. Or too new. Or don't know what I'm doing. Or am frustrated. Or I've tried and never get anywhere. Or I haven't dated since I was in my twenties. How does it work anyway?"

If what you've always done isn't taking you where you want to go, it's time to make some changes.

Women in All Decades

Time and time again, women in all decades ask the same questions and have the same worries about how to date, where to find him, and how to keep him. The difference being as you get older the baggage can be bigger, and heavier and usually involves more people. Crazy ex's, multiple ex's, kids from multiple previous marriages (or not marriages), and even pets. There's also geography in the mix if the ex and the kids live in a different state or even another country. There may be joint businesses, retirement accounts, and multiple homes. (Untangling all of that is tricky so I hope your lawyer and financial advisor were really good.)

Yet, even with a deeper degree of complication, your fundamental *dating age* comes down to your own experience, steering clear of the *B.A.T. Signs and Types,* learning about yourself, figuring out what you want, and how to recognize it. Oh ya, and what to do when you find it.

Consistently, a common flaw is starting with *"how* do I date" and *"who he* should be," before you understand the answers to *"who* I am," *"what* do I want," and *"why* do I want to date."

5

Journal Moments

Advancing your *dating age* is fundamentally about discovering yourself. To help you explore, jot down a few thoughts in a journal as you read this book. Ask yourself some tough questions and have the courage to answer them honestly. You may not be sure what questions to ask, so I've provided some for you in each chapter. Feel free to expand on my questions with your own.

There are no right answers, and "I don't know" is an honest answer at this point as long as you're open to learning the answer. If you aren't, "I don't know" just becomes a fearful cop out and will keep you stuck exactly where you are. Your journal could be a special notebook, a diary, or a password protected file on your computer. Whatever is most comfortable for you is the one to choose.

Be careful of automatic answers, feeling like it must be an "appropriate" answer, and ignoring that little voice in your head that gave you the real answer. You don't get extra credit for punctuation, spelling or even using complete sentences. Don't edit yourself. Just let the thoughts and emotions come to you.

Your journal provides a private avenue to explore your feelings, beliefs, emotions, values, assumptions and way of thinking as you experience dating and relationships. As you continue to date, come back to the *Journal Moment* questions and update your answers. Learning about yourself is where success begins, and how it continues.

Date or Relationship

One very important distinction is the difference between a *date* and a *relationship*. Going out with someone once is a date, not a relationship or life long commitment. Even going out with him a few times is still *dating*, not a relationship. Don't view the first few dates as "forever," simply view them as a fun opportunity to see if you'd like to spend time with him again. Be truly present with *this* man right now, and very careful of assuming he is or isn't like your last man (or husband) and acting as if he'll do or won't do things just like the last guy.

Make the first few dates short, keep it light and have a good time. It's a nice evening, lunch or maybe a drink. (If you choose to drink, be sure to keep your wits about you.) You go home (by yourself) and reflect on if you'd like to see him again. That's the only question you need to answer after a first meeting, or even a second. We'll get to going home with him and having sex in the next chapter.

Yes, you can dream about becoming Mrs. Man I Just Met, though be careful of getting ahead of yourself. Dreaming about him and staring into space with a grin on your face is important, but part of the dating journey is learning some *Basic Facts* about him, along with experiencing how he lives and runs his life. The butterflies in your stomach when you're around him don't tell you if you can build a life together. *Good decisions involve your head and your heart.* Much more about those decisions later.

How You'll Know Better This Time

Living on purpose is one of the ways you'll know better this time. Consider your life and relationships – do you *Live Deliberately* or *Live By Default*?

Living Deliberately means you know yourself, have learned from your past, stand in your own power and believe in your decisions. *Living by Default* is an auto-pilot attitude where you've never reflected on your past, defined standards for yourself or the relationships in your life, nor made any changes to improve your situation, whatever that may be.

The next two sections give some common attitudes, approaches to life, and choices in dating or relationships based on *Living by Default* or *Living Deliberately*.

Living by Default

‣ You tend to run on auto-pilot, going in the same direction and doing the same things you've always done before. Maybe complaining how things never change though never choosing to change things.

‣ You let other people define what you want in your life in general as well as your love life.

‣ You nit pick about who your man should be, yet haven't explored your own character yet. Seems you are more concerned about him and what's wrong with him than what's right with you.

‣ You bulldoze forward and focus on how you'll get something without regard for *why* you want it.

‣ You choose to date, and maybe even keep, whatever man shows up.

Living Deliberately

‣ You've defined some priorities, desires and what's important to you.

‣ Whether you like change or not, you recognize its part of life and can adapt when necessary.

‣ You take time to reflect on the outcomes of the decisions you've made in the interest of learning something useful this time.

‣ You are aware of the factors and emotions impacting your choices.

‣ You consider *why* you want something and how it helps you create what you want in your life.

‣ You choose *Mr. Right for You* and you know why.

You Don't Know What You Don't Know

Whatever your reaction to the *Deliberate or Default* description, it's ok. We're at the beginning of *creating deliberate change* in your love life.

The *impact* of *Living Deliberately* or *Living By Default* centers on the *reasons* behind the decisions you make. Many times, you don't know what you don't know until you've taken time to reflect on what's already happened and look ahead to what you want your life and relationships to become. Perhaps you'll discover some hidden motivators for your past decisions, and learn something you can use today and in the future to live more deliberately. As I said earlier, *good decisions involve the common sense of your head and the emotions of your heart.*

It's a Process

Have patience with yourself. Getting divorced, dumped, or starting over for any of a multitude of reasons only means things are going to change and you can take a different road. Choose a different path. Create another life for yourself. This is a process so let yourself evolve through it without expectations of acing the test right now. Fear is a natural emotion in this journey – rejection is very real and will happen. Failure is possible. So is success. Risk seeps into every choice. Believe you deserve love from a good man and have faith in yourself. Yes, change is scary though it can be exciting if you *have the courage to let it become an adventure.*

What Will You Choose?

Default

‣ Continue as you have.

‣ Stay where you're comfy, stuck right where you are.

‣ Unwilling to see yourself and your life from a new perspective.

Deliberate

‣ Recognize your learning stage and *dating age.*

‣ Make your own choices.

‣ Be smart and choose to do things differently.

This Time

At the end of each chapter you'll find a group of affirming statements. Use them as encouragement when you need it or to celebrate making *deliberate decisions* that are good for you. Say them to yourself, say them out loud, or write them down in your journal. Whatever is most impactful for you to remember these promises to yourself and the changes you're making *this time.*

‣ *I accept my dating age, whatever that may be, and vow to begin from here. I can do this.*

‣ *I'll have patience with myself as I experience the dating process, make mistakes, learn from them and try again.*

CHAPTER 2

Stuff No One Will Tell You 'Cause They Don't Know Either

There are some taboo topics in dating. (And people wonder why they are confused.) The first one is what's inside women's *Cinderella Head* and how it's used to justify idiotic behavior from a man. Discussing sex, having sex, or not having sex is another taboo topic, especially when it comes to discussing it with the man you are seeing, even though it's on your mind. *Friends with Benefits* is a particular scenario related to having sex or not and with whom. First we start with women's *Cinderella Heads*.

Cinderella Head

Few women escape the programming that starts at the beginning of our lives: be a princess and wait for prince charming to come and rescue us. What we're being rescued from is still a mystery, though I am certainly a product of that belief, and those experiences. When I was in pre-school, I remember a birthday party where my "boyfriend" and I were sitting on the back patio watching all the other "children" play. We were playing house – a game that simulates what we are "supposed" to do as adults. He was sitting in his kid sized lawn chair being the husband, and I was sitting in a kid sized reclining lawn chair being the wife. Nothing wrong with playing house. Nothing wrong with sitting on the back porch with your husband for that matter.

The programming issues surface as they translate into expectations and beliefs that women don't have a life unless we're in a relationship. Like we're not whole unless we can say we have a man which creates tendencies to let just any man in our lives. Especially since the programming continues with an underlying idea that relationships begin with a woman wanting the man, and the man needing to be *conquered* into a commitment. Mix all that together and we justify idiotic behavior from a man who isn't worthy of our attention.

The *He's Different* Syndrome

Our *Cinderella Head* creates this condition. I've heard it from friends, watch it happen repeatedly among women I've met, and have done it to myself. We meet a man who is a *Bad Ass Trouble B.A.T.* and do everything we can to convince ourselves he is worth being around. Worth spending our time on. Worth putting up with his ridiculous behavior because he's "a man" and that's "just how they are."

The worse he treats us the more we convince ourselves he must be "the one." So it doesn't matter he never has time for you, only calls at the last minute and expects you to be at his beck and call, never asks about you or is concerned about your well being, or only talks about what *he* needs. We're secretly thinking, or more likely acting as if "I'll be the one he wants to change his wayward ways for, and commit to, and he'll stop being a jerk 'cause *he's different* than the other men who are jerks… I'll be the one he'll suddenly want to come home to and become the good man for (just like in the movies)."

So you continue to date him and allow his shenanigans in your life. In reality, the only changing this *B.A.T.* will do is if it benefits him or makes it easier to get what he wants out of you. And, likely, in your *Cinderella Head* dream land – the only changing you do is to adapt to his demands and become someone you're not. The irony is you're now convinced you and he are headed for a fairy tale ending - except he's headed out the door. I'm guessing that's not the way it worked in your dream land.

All He Said was "Hello"

Another *Cinderella Head* moment is when a man says "hello" and we create an entire love story from it, tell all of our friends and get them to help us analyze how he said it, where we were, what we were wearing, and if we were having a good hair day. Stop already. Absolutely enjoy the moment and the memories of it though don't put more pressure on it, or yourself.

"Hello" isn't a marriage proposal. It's not even an invitation for a date. Yes, it's a good place to start, though keep your dreamy head in check otherwise it'll ooze out your pores and shower desperate all over him. *Desperate* is the *most effective date repellent ever.*

Pay Attention

It's time to pay attention to your decisions and dig deep into the reasons you make them. *Mr. He's Different* isn't suddenly going change his ways and become a man you deserve. You aren't wearing glass slippers for him to find. You are an intelligent, successful, smart woman and you deserve a man who already knows how to treat women. Without tactics. Without wishing. And without *Cinderella Head* justification.

A Journal Moment

‣ What *Cinderella Head* moments have you observed in your life? Choices? Relationships?

‣ Have you found yourself thinking "I can't be alone." Or, "He's better than nothing?"

‣ Are there moments where "desperate" might have oozed out of you?

Sex – To Do It or Not To Do It

As for sex…that's always a touchy subject. The biggest issue with this topic is no one wants to talk about it. And, if they do it's in a hushed whisper like we're going to get arrested or something for daring to utter the word. Talking about sex is absolutely required in dating and relationships yet no one wants to because you are worried about what it means, or doesn't mean, that *you* brought up the topic.

Women are worried if they do or don't want to talk about it, they may be perceived in one extreme or the other – the prude or the slut. Yet, if men bring it up, it's expected and ok with us because "they are men." Have you ever dated a man who actually wanted to talk about sex before he did it with you? If so, that's a sign of a maturity. Regardless of whether he wanted or expected the same things regarding sex as you, if he's honest enough to be open about it, respect him for it. If your values and his don't match up, it's over and you can both move on.

Make it Simple

Regardless of who wants to talk about it or who doesn't, the decision to do it should be very simple. If you want to do it – do it. If you don't – don't. Don't let him use it as an excuse to "move things forward" if you aren't ready to take that step. Would you let your teenage daughter's boyfriend get away with that? Then you shouldn't either.

Discussing expectations about sex in a relationship is a sign of maturity. It's also a sign you are both interested in a relationship. Avoiding the subject could mean he isn't actually interested in anything serious. Or, avoiding the topic could mean he's uncomfortable because of his own issues and beliefs about it being something that "isn't discussed."

If he keeps kissing you while simultaneously avoiding the conversation, it's likely he's just avoiding the subject because he doesn't want anything serious and he's hoping you'll just cave in and have some fun. If he's wildly nervous, seems to like you, and doesn't exhibit the *B.A.T. Signs*, maybe you give him a break and approach the subject another day. (I didn't say go ahead and hop into bed with him.) Of course, other things to consider are the practice of safe sex, your health, and your partner's health. The bottom line is if he won't talk about it, regardless of the reason, he doesn't deserve to do it with you.

One more note – if *you* are wildly nervous about the topic or avoiding it because you just want to have some fun… consider which one is your motivation. You don't want him to use you, so don't use him. If you're wildly nervous, maybe it's because it's too early in the dating process with him to discuss it yet. Nothing wrong with waiting. Also nothing wrong with hopping into bed if that's what you both want and you understand the *mutual expectations*.

Setting the Expectations about Sex

Before we address how you bring up the subject, let's first clarify what "setting expectations" means. Things get really uncomfortable if you have sex without knowing what each of you is expecting, then wonder what it means for days or weeks afterwards. Could it still work out? Maybe, though it'll be harder on both of you, and I'd guess the more time that passes neither of you will want to ask the question. You may both be wondering if the other is monogamous or how many other sexual partners are involved. Most likely, you're both making assumptions and it's possible they aren't the same ones. This sounds like avoiding the conversation because you're both chicken and don't want to establish any expectations, which probably means you aren't ready to "define" anything. All that adds up to casual dating where you are having sex too.

Talking about expectations is one way to resolve this ambiguous place where you are both making assumptions. For you, having sex may mean automatic monogamy. For him, it may not. For you, it may mean you aren't seeing anyone else so there's monogamy in the bedroom plus exclusivity in dating. (Yes, those could be separate questions.) For him it may only mean he got laid and has a date with someone else tomorrow. Or, for some women – maybe you are the one who wants to get laid and he isn't ready. Or he wants monogamy and you don't. Talking about expectations is the key to being on the same page about this.

A Journal Moment

Of course, before you have a conversation with him you need to know your own expectations and what you want relative to sex on dates or in a relationship. A few questions to help sort out your feelings:

▸ Do you want sex to fulfill something physical, or connect emotionally?

▸ What should have already happened for you to feel comfortable having sex on a date?

▸ What is the role of sex on a date?

▸ What should have already happened for you to feel comfortable having sex in a relationship?

▸ What is the role of sex in a relationship?

▸ Are you looking for monogamy or do you feel ok if he sleeps with you and sleeps with other women?

Clarify the Conversation about Sex

Just to be clear, the conversation I'm referencing, and the expectations to set with each other, is not about discussing what you like in bed. That's a different discussion you should have at some point when you are in a relationship. I'm talking about getting naked in the first place and what that means for you and for him.

This conversation about sex only matters if you want a relationship or if you are concerned about his feelings. If all you want is something casual and you're choosing not to care about his feelings, hop in the sac and have a good time. Just remember the consequences to treating people that way. You don't want to be used, so don't use him.

If you want something with potential – have the conversation. You'll learn if you both see potential in pursuing something more with each other and want to take things to the next level. Unfortunately, if one of you sees the potential and the other doesn't, it's most likely over.

An important note - You can't ask "What does this mean?" immediately after you have sex with him, or even on the same night. That's just needy and clingy and kills the moment. If you are worried about what it means, or what it doesn't mean, you need to have the conversation about expectations *before* you have sex. It needs to be at a time when you are out to lunch or spending time together when it has nothing to do with sex. It'll be much easier to share from your head and your heart, and not be distracted by other parts of your anatomy.

As for the women who need to know if he is skilled in the bedroom before you decide if you want to date him…that's dangerous ground. You don't want him to dump you because of the sex… or right after the sex… or give the impression he's using you. So why would you treat him that way? He might be just the man of character you want, yet treating him like a piece of meat will likely mean he's gone.

What You Want Versus How You Act

If you want something serious and you are approaching it with a very casual attitude, don't be surprised when it turns out to be casual. Don't be surprised after you hop into bed without a word about expectations, but with a relationship as your goal, and find he's thinking, "Fun. Without obligation."

I am not judging or saying you should want things to be casual or things to be serious, yet if you approach sex with a casual attitude, without conversation, and jump into bed thinking it'll become something… just understand it may not. At a very basic level, if you are a woman who wants something serious and you casually had sex - what you want and how you are behaving don't match. They don't jive. Your casual sexual behavior doesn't match your "serious relationship" desire.

There is an element of "serious" in a "serious" relationship where the role of sex takes on a more intimate feel that includes an emotional attachment. In a casual relationship, sex is just part of the dating road to what you're *hoping* will become something serious. So – read between the lines. YOU become part of the road. You become "on the way" to something you're *hoping* is serious.

If you're looking for something that could become a real relationship and not just a casual thing, be an adult and have the conversation. I didn't say it would be a breeze to do, or that you'll feel comfortable doing it. Though the more you believe in what you want and respect yourself enough to discuss it, the easier it will become. I believe you can do it if you choose to. This isn't something to chat about on the first date... unless it becomes clear it's necessary. Most likely, it's after you've been out with him a few times, things seem to be going well, and he's someone you want to continue seeing.

Mixed Signals About Sex

By the way, giving mixed signals about sex really bugs men... well it bugs the men who have scruples. The men who are B.A.T.s just see mixed signals as a challenge to find out if they can get in your pants. Make up your mind about what sex means to you, behave accordingly and stay true to your values. Of course, if you are playing games with him, you may be the B.A.T..

How Do I Bring Up the Topic of Sex?

You may be wondering how on earth you could bring up this subject. The good news is it'll come up at some point - especially if you like each other, enjoy holding hands and making out. In reality, the best time to talk about it is when you're discussing what you're looking for in a relationship. Are you casually dating yet aren't seeing anyone in particular? Are you looking to find someone special and date only him? Are you just having some fun and not interested in connecting with anyone – just living in the moment? And what does he want?

As you continue to date, and it hasn't come up yet, it will. You may get an idea of his attitude based on his cavalier behavior toward you and his "in the moment" approach to dating. Or, you'll notice his deliberate behavior to treat you well and care for your needs.

One specific moment is when you are sharing stories of past relationships. That's an easier time to talk about how you feel about sex and what it means to you given you are already discussing past experiences with each other. Remember you can ask him questions too. It's not just about you sharing what you want; it's about him sharing his values with you too. Scared it may feel like you are standing on eggshells during this conversation? You'll get better at it the more you believe in what you want and why.

Note: Avoid talking about the past when you first meet or on the first few dates. Too much talk about the past is a turn off and leaves him to wonder if you are interested in the present, interested in him, or just living in the past. The reverse is true too – if he's spends a lot of time talking about the past – you should be wondering if he's interested in the present, interested in you, or still living the past.

Another opportunity to bring up the expectations about sex is if he's kissing you and clearly wants to move on and you don't. This isn't a recommended moment, though if you've let other opportunities pass by and still haven't talked yet, it could be a last resort.

So, simply stop him and tell him you want to slow things down. Ask him if you could talk about sex sometime and the expectations of each of you before you go any further. And don't make it that night.

He's not thinking clearly and neither are you if you've been smooching and he's a good kisser.

This won't be a popular moment by the way. Especially if he was under the impression you were giving all green lights and are ready to round the bases so to speak. Best if you talk about it in a more of matter-of-fact moment, as part of the conversation about what you want from a relationship and how long you want to wait.

If he's kissing you and you want to have sex then he'll be looking for the green light to proceed. If you want to round the bases, then keep the light green. If you don't, you can stop - *regardless* of what base you are on. Of course, if you're giving him red lights and he's trying to proceed anyway, kick him out, leave or call the cops. And no, don't see him again. He's not suddenly going to become less creepy overnight.

Won't Talking About Sex Scare Him Off?

If it does, it just means you and he aren't a match. You have different values. You're worth waiting for. If *you're* using the assumption that he'll be "scared off" as an *excuse* to get laid, maybe you are the horny one who doesn't want to wait and you're conveniently blaming it on him. Just remember what was said earlier about deciding what you want and having your behavior match.

How Long Should I Wait to Have Sex?

A very popular dating question is "How long should I wait before having sex?" Only you can answer what feels right for you. Just be very clear with yourself on how you feel about the subject, actually going through with it, and how you'll feel the next morning. Journaling about the previous questions should help you sort this out.

Traditionalists will say wait until marriage and make an argument asking why would he buy the cow (marry you) when he can get the milk (sex) for free (without a marital commitment). Progressive thinkers and women who enjoy sex will say they want to sample the goods before they buy, so to speak. Does he have skills? Is he teachable? Are you? Do you have the same idea about the role of sex in a relationship and are you both of the same mindset about experimentation and what you enjoy?

Generally speaking, men are ready way before we are and once they get you into bed, their motivation changes. Doesn't mean they stop caring. Doesn't mean you'll breakup. Well, be sure to read the *B.A.T. Signs* chapter on these issues. It could mean all of those things actually. It does mean the date… er relationship… er date… just changed, dramatically. Until you are in a relationship – it's most likely just a date. If you want sex on your date, enjoy yourself. Just don't be surprised if your *Cinderella Head* fantasy of you two "making love" doesn't add up to fireworks and diamonds. Might be you only had sex.

Whatever you decide you want, have a conversation about it first. Oh my… I can hear some of you thinking… why??? Why do we have to plan this?? It kills the mystery. The romance. The passion. Perhaps having a conversation could be construed as "planning" sex, though again it's about setting an expectation, not putting sex on your calendar. More importantly, it's about discussing *mutual* expectations.

If you are seeing someone and want a relationship with him, my suggestion is to wait awhile. I've heard everything from 5 to 10 dates or 1 to 2 months. The sooner there's sex, the sooner the expectations from each other change. And, the sooner it all becomes way more complicated than maybe it needs to be. Doesn't matter how simple you try to make it – sex always makes things more complicated. Always.

Just get comfortable with what you want relative to sex… to do it… or not to do it. It's still your call.

Friends with Benefits (FWB)

On a date, you're either learning if there's a romantic interest, or you already know there is one. In a relationship, you know there's a romantic, emotional attachment. In a *Friends with Benefits* situation, you may appreciate him as a person, and for his skills in the bedroom, though there's no romantic emotional attachment for either of you. You don't date or have any commitment to each other. There's no assumption of monogamy. It's sex. For the purpose of sex and some version of physical contact with a "friend" whom you trust.

Sometimes the friend is actually a friend of yours. Sometimes the friend is someone you met and you chose to make this arrangement. Be very clear about what you want from this friendship. Know yourself well enough to understand how you'll feel if he's sleeping with you and sleeping with other women too.

The FWB Problem

The problem comes when you or your FWB develop deeper feelings that aren't mutual. Then you're in trouble. Now, your friendship has been compromised because you complicated it by adding sex. If you want to date someone then date him and don't kid yourself into a FWB arrangement.

A huge warning is when you decide to have a *Friends with Benefits* arrangement with a man in hopes of it changing into a relationship. Could it happen? It's possible, though that isn't the expectation you've set with him so don't be surprised if he doesn't share your feelings. FWB is like short term parking. There's no long term pass to stay or return - just a place to park while you get what you want at the moment.

Can You Handle It?

Some women can handle this type of casual interaction. Some can't. Know which one you are. If you decide to try it, yet aren't sure if this scenario is for you, watch for warnings of justification. Be aware of disappointment when you ask him to do "date like" stuff and he turns you down. Or, you're peeved because he doesn't ask you to do date like stuff. Watch yourself when you start saying, "Well, I'm sleeping with him... you'd think he would...." Remember, he's a FWB, not a date. He doesn't need to take you out or buy you flowers.

Also beware of over analyzing everything that happens between the two of you, yet you are still convincing yourself it's "just casual." If it's actually casual, it doesn't take a lot of thought. If it bugs you enough to think about it all the time, over analyze your conversations with him, or otherwise obsess about if you are doing things together and when – that sounds like your emotions are involved and you wish his were too.

I have heard stories where a man and woman agree to a FWB arrangement and choose monogamy under the premise that neither really wants to date though they'd like to have safe sex in their life. The warnings were everywhere. She wanted him to be her date for a wedding and was peeved when he said no. Seriously? Going to a wedding with a FWB? He could've gone, yet that sounds like a date not a FWB. Again, it's about expectations. If you want to date him, date him. Don't settle for a FWB scenario.

What Will You Choose?

Default	Deliberate
‣ Continue to justify idiotic behavior from him or in you.	‣ Examine your Cinderella Head tendencies.
‣ Ignoring the obvious - him treating you badly.	‣ Stop tolerating idiotic behavior in him or in you.
‣ Denying how you truly feel about sex on a date or in a relationship.	‣ Believe in yourself and your values related to sex.

This Time

As a reminder - Use these affirming statements as encouragement when you need it or to celebrate deliberate changes you're making *this time.*

‣ *I will keep my Cinderella Head tendencies in check and remember good decisions involve the common sense from my head and the emotions in my heart.*

‣ *I will figure out what sex means to me and behave in a way that's consistent with my beliefs.*

‣ *Before I engage in a FWB, I'll figure out if that's what I really want from him.*

CHAPTER 3

Your Real Friends

Support from your girlfriends is crucial to life in general, though especially for your love life. They are who you cry to, who you laugh with, who will bring you chocolate if things go wrong, and who will help you celebrate when things go right. Girlfriend relationships require effort and appreciation just like romantic ones, though they will still be there for you when he isn't. Treat them well, help them when they need you, and don't blow them off for a date.

Listening to your friends, keeping them in your priorities, and letting them help you creates a significant support system. Understand the difference between a *real friend* who will tell you the truth, a *broken friend* who means well, and a *cheering friend* who tells you what you want to hear. All three are important though they have different perspectives on your life and dating decisions.

Your girlfriends are also a crucial part of an often overlooked part of dating – your personal safety. No one wants to talk about the possibility you are meeting a real creep, yet it could happen. Be smart and ask your friends to make the very important *security call* that's explained below. They want you to be happy and safe.

The Value of a Real Friend

The very best *real friends* you can have are those who *give each other permission to bring up the toughest topics and have a frank conversation*. Part of the agreement is no judgment, no pictures, and total confidentiality including no posts to any social media sites. This allows complete honesty and trust where you can be open, ask for help, or dig into whatever needs to be addressed.

If your *real friends* have something honest to say about your dating choices, you should hear them out. Don't be defensive or get your hackles up. Just listen and find out why they are sharing what they have to say.

Perspective

It's your life to live and that never changes, though when you're immersed in the emotional confusion (good or bad) of a situation, a *real friend* can help you see things more clearly. They can take the emotion out of the situation and give you an outside perspective. It's why businesses hire consultants, professional athletes hire coaches, and why you ask your real friends if your butt looks fat in those jeans.

Asking for help doesn't mean you've failed, it means you are smart enough to recognize you don't have all the answers. You're looking for recommendations, advice, and observations from an "outsider" who isn't neck deep in the situation and can see things you can't. So while you are all giddy and giggling over this man, real friends are noticing things about him you aren't and see *B.A.T. Signs* you miss. It's important you listen to them. Given your real friends are probably the best ones to spot *B.A.T. Signs* for you, be sure they read this book too. (Even if they are married.)

Will you always agree with your real friends' opinion? Nope. Not saying that. What I am saying is you owe it to yourself to listen, consider what they observe, and why they are sharing it. It's not to hurt or judge you. Quite the contrary. Real friends want each other to have the best life possible.

Honesty

Real friends tell you the truth even when you don't want to hear it. We all need friends who will tell us things we don't want to know or acknowledge and they love us through it anyway. We've had our moments with the ugly, yet loved sweater or the funny hat or the wrong hair color.

Your *real friends* won't judge your lapse in fashion sense; they'll kindly share an opinion that perhaps the color or style doesn't do you justice. Did her comment mean you needed to change your clothes? Maybe, depends upon if you agree with her and if you respect her fashion sense. The more difficult examples might be help with the kids, caring for aging parents, or buying a house. *Real friends* are there for you through all of it with their support and with their honesty.

As for your love life, what they have to say about your choices may not be very flattering. It's risky ground for both of you. She's out on a limb with concern for you, and if you don't agree with her, you both risk the friendship. If you truly are real friends, you'll work through disagreements about men and still be in each other's corner.

Tips for Your Real Friends

If you are a *real friend* for someone, be careful your genuine intention to help isn't masked by how you go about it. If she isn't ready to listen to reason, no amount of talking, emails or booze will change it. The best approach is to ask her questions about what she wants, how she wants to live and let her compare it to what she has. *Listen* to the answers and *don't say a word*. Don't judge her or tell her what to do. You know she needs to make the decision for herself so be cautious of your own frustration showing.

You likely see the problems and the answers to her current situation, whatever it is, though she may not. Help her discover them with your heartfelt care, perspective and honesty. It's what she needs from you.

Broken Friends

If your friends are struggling through their own life issues or a breakup or divorce, they have their own concerns to contend with. Perhaps you should love them where they are, but take their advice as it is given--from someone who is broken (hopefully temporarily). This emotional state doesn't make them bad people, just doesn't make them the best people to provide help for you.

If you are in a "broken" place in your life like recovering from a breakup, getting advice from your "broken" friends is a little like the blind leading the blind. Having them to commiserate with will feel comforting so accept their support, hugs and beverage of your choice. Just be careful not to let them hold you back and keep you broken.

Now is the time to consider who you trust, the advice you receive and from whom. Don't take their competitive jabs or pay attention to their envious scowl when they realize you're learning faster than they are, or they realize they are stuck and aren't learning at all. That's just fear about their own lives rearing its ugly head and taking aim at you. That's about them, not about you. Love them where they are and recognize when to walk away and talk another day.

Of course, most people are better at giving advice than managing their own lives; even when they know they should be following their own advice. So it's possible your broken friends still have insight for you to learn from, though be sure to surround yourself with healthy friends too. More broken friends than healthy friends can really stunt your growth because you feed off each other and focus on all the negative frustration and anger instead of choosing what you want this time.

Who You Spend Time With

You want to learn and grow. If some friends don't support your growth, or don't want to grow themselves, maybe spend less time with them and spend more time with friends who do support the changes you are making in your life. It's important to surround yourself with emotionally healthy, level-headed and encouraging people during your relationship transition, or any life transition for that matter. It's a deliberate choice to help you stay focused on what you want and the great things you deserve in life.

Now healthy is relative, and even emotionally healthy people have their issues and moments of instability. It's part of being human. The difference I see between being healthy or not is being aware of your own issues and doing something to address them.

The most hazardous people are those who have issues and don't know it. Or they do know it and deny it or ignore it. They are still stuck in the "blame everyone else" state where nothing is ever their problem or a result of their own choices. Needless to say, blaming everyone else for your own life isn't a healthy state of mind. If you are one of these people, it's time to make different decisions.

Who Has Your Back?

Surround yourself with people who have your back, not just those who will tell you what you want to hear. Friends who cheer for you, always agree with whatever you say, and want you to be happy all mean well. The issue is they wouldn't tell you the truth about the spinach in your teeth or if they are concerned about how the man you are dating treats you. Seems they will talk about it with other friends and totally avoid talking about it with you. It isn't that they don't care – they just don't care enough to "go there" or "cause a conflict" or more likely "risk having you mad at them."

Caution

It's far easier to find friends who will cheer for you, tell you everything is ok, help you justify his bad behavior with "he's a man" reasoning, tell you "I'm sure he'll call…" when it's apparent he won't, and look past the obvious *B.A.T. Signs* he's showing. It's an unfortunate reality that these friends and acquaintances are more abundant than those who will sit you down with a reality check… and it spells trouble for you.

If you're already dating, spending time with friends who avoid any conflict means it's far easier to stay in the all-men-are-the-problem attitude as you're surrounded by friends who buy into that thinking. If you are newer to dating, this means you're at risk of developing that attitude and the resulting pattern of choosing *B.A.T.s* to date - much to your detriment.

They've Been There

Your *real friends* have your back because they understand what it's like to go through some of life's crap and have learned how to cope. More importantly, they have taken time to examine their role in it and have learned something to improve their lives. This experience gives them perspective you don't have when you are neck deep in the emotion of your dating life. Doesn't mean your real friends don't have their broken moments or aren't interested in cheering for you. It's that they care enough to share the truth while they are cheering, and tell you what you *need* to hear, not necessarily what you *want* to hear.

Choose those who will support you with honesty and love, and believe you deserve the best. That creates a support system to help you grow.

A Journal Moment

Consider the friends you spend the most time with.
- Are they people you go to with the really tough problems?
- Do you have someone who will "say it like it is" with your best interest at heart?

Signals Your Friends are Worried

A signal your friends are concerned with your dating choice is if they dodge spending time with the two of you. Or maybe it's the raised eyebrow whenever you mention his name or the blatant change of subject if you start telling a story about him. That's avoiding. Might want to investigate what's going on and why they feel this way. Could be you talk about him non-stop and they'd like to discuss something else. Could be they are wondering about something related to him and are trying to figure out how to approach the subject. Best to find out what's up.

If you evade your friends when they ask about who you are dating… that's not a good indication either. Assuming you have friends you respect and have your best interest at heart – why wouldn't you want to share info about who you are interested in? What don't you want them to know? Something is up if you are clamming up.

His Response to Your Real Friends

Another side of your real friends is his response to them. If he isolates you from them it's a sign he knows your friends don't like him, perhaps because they can see right through him. So, instead of forging a relationship with them (that would be the mature thing to do), he keeps you from them. Another thing he may do is avoid participating in anything involving them. And, he doesn't include them in any group activities like meeting for dinner or going to a ballgame.

He thinks (or he knows) he isn't worthy, so instead of showing your friends he is worthy, he manipulates the situation and keeps you apart. Could be he's just a jerk and he's isolating you because he doesn't care about spending time with your friends. Might be a combination of being a jerk and not being worthy. Another possibility is he's not planning to stick around very long.

The really bad part is if you go along with him instead of your friends who love you. He's new to your life! Why would you let him in your life and ignore the people who've been there for you through thick and thin?

Giving Up Friends

There are situations where friendships change to the point you let them go. And I don't mean you're tired of their common sense reasoning and spotting *B.A.T. Signs* in the men you date so you stop spending time with them. That would be you avoiding the truth.

I mean your life has changed and either they aren't the support you need at this point in your life (or maybe you aren't what they need), or it's a tough situation brought on by the end of a relationship – most likely a long-term one or a marriage.

When you've spent a lot of years in a marriage or relationship, you've both made new friends, and shared other friends. And, now that you are single, the friends are changing. The relationships are changing. Perhaps you've already noticed some of your friends are "his friends" now. Maybe some are "your friends." You may have even experienced this during the divorce or breakup. Your entire social circle changed the moment the decision was made to end the relationship, regardless of whether you wanted it or he did.

Here's the thing – your friends may not know what to do either. Depending upon how and why the relationship ended, they may be torn about who to "affiliate" with. Who do they get to hang out with now? Maybe they love you both, yet feel like they have to take sides. And they really don't want to be in the middle. They may also feel threatened by the fact your relationship ended. Perhaps you were the "perfect couple" and it's over. So now it's the talk of the neighborhood. And, your friends are worried if it could happen to you two….. "Oh no… it could happen to me." Like it's contagious or something.

So, here's what you do. Talk to them. Share your feelings about the situation and ask about theirs. You are in a different place in life now. Some friendships will continue. Some you'll need to let go of. Some will become your real friends and some, you may discover, always have been.

Be Smart About Safety

Another reality check your friends can help with: Use your head and be smart about safety. In the beginning, this is a date, with someone new to your life, regardless of how you met him. You don't know this man. Do not let him pick you up at your house, tell him where you live, or what car you drive. Meet him in a public place with a well lit parking lot. Always tell one of your real friends where and when you're going, who you are meeting, and how you met.

Security Call

Ask your friend to give you a "security call" during the first 30-45 minutes of the date. This accomplishes two things: 1) checks you are ok, and 2) gives you an excuse to leave if you aren't. If you are uncomfortable with him (in a creepy way, not the I'm-so-nervous-I'm-shaking way), then make an excuse and leave. Remember, the general rules of safety and awareness we women follow every day don't go away because you are out on a date.

Don't obsess about this stuff, though do take it very seriously. Your gut will know if he's creepy and dating is a good time to start listening to it. A tell tale warning is if he follows you to the bathroom and it's not an "I also need to go" moment, it feels like a "you're keeping watch on me" moment. Ick. Leave. And, don't let him follow you to your car.

Another creepy warning is if he's pushy and asks a lot of questions about where you spend your time and when you're there. Is he nervous, curious and trying to learn about you? Maybe. Is he a creepy stalker? Maybe. Again - listen to your instincts.

Could you use text messages instead of a phone call? Yes, though use code words. If he is a creepy stalker he could have taken your phone and easily respond or text your friend that everything is fine. Use a code with her so only she knows the words that mean "I'm ok" or "I'm not." Also have a rule you both reply to text messages so there's no question they are sent and received while you are on your date.

What If I Like Him and He's Not Creepy?

If you are getting along, and are comfortable with him, take a moment during the conversation and tell him you are expecting a call from one of your friends and you need to take it. You could say something like, "I'm having a great time… Just in case something unusual happened I asked one of my friends to call me. So sorry for the interruption."

Be sure to apologize for the phone call that is about to happen, and take the call in front of him so he knows it's not an excuse to escape. Don't be shocked if the look on his face is a bit surprised. His pride and ego are on the line in this moment so smile and be sincere. This isn't a game I'm asking you to play. It's for your safety. Don't worry, men who are paying attention to what it must be like to date in this day and age will understand and appreciate you take care of yourself.

You Must Answer the Phone

You must answer the phone when your friend calls. Otherwise, your friend will wonder if you not answering the phone is a good or very bad thing. Let her know if you need her to call you again. Of course, if you feel the need for her to call you again, you should probably just leave the first time.

You could use text messages though be sure you say something to him just as if she was calling. Otherwise, he just sees you texting in front of him and wondering what you are up to instead of paying attention to him. Remember, in this scenario, you like him, are getting along well and aren't getting any creep vibes from him. So, explaining why you are on your phone is being respectful. Yes, being on your phone during a date is incredibly rude, though this security call is the only exception barring any other type of emergency.

Reality Check

At some point during the dating and relationship building process, and it is a process, you'll become more comfortable with your own choices and the *reasons you make them.* Life tends to ebb and flow and so does what you learn about yourself and your relationships. Part of growing is recognizing when you are regressing to old habits, and old *B.A.T.* choices. Another part is when you are forging into unknown territory and learning new things. Your real friends are one of the keys to a reality check and putting things into perspective.

A word of caution - Be aware of the pace you're learning. Remember your relative experience in dating and relationships may be small. I've heard many times, "He's the most wonderful man I've ever met!" That may be true. Yet if the pool of men you've dated totals three, it's not hard to get one that's better than two others. See my point?

I love hearing that comment because it means you are growing and starting to recognize differences in the men you are choosing. Taking some time to reflect on the decision could mean you are moving closer to what you want. A reality check from your real friends could help you stay on the path.

What Will You Choose?

Default	Deliberate
‣ Stubbornly decide you know best and aren't willing to listen to anyone else's perspective.	‣ Reflect on your circle of friends and understand who's the best support for you.
‣ Choose to commiserate with your broken friends and avoid growing with your real friends.	‣ Listen to your real friends' concerns.
	‣ Recognize decisions are still yours.
‣ Ignore your own safety.	‣ Schedule security calls and follow security suggestions.

This Time

Use these affirming statements as encouragement when you need it or to celebrate deliberate changes you're making *this time.*

‣ *I appreciate the outside perspective my real friends can give me and will listen even when I don't want to hear it. I know it's still my life and my choices to make.*

‣ *I love my broken friends and will help them grow if they choose.*

‣ *I will let go of friendships if necessary because I realize its part of life's journey.*

‣ *I'll be smart about my own personal safety.*

CHAPTER 4

Drama Queen

There's a silent issue many women have and don't even realize its part of their life and personality. If you're afflicted with this it's so natural to you, you don't recognize you have it, do it, or even that *it's a problem*. It's become the core of life's decisions, including the men you date, the relationships you create, and situations you *allow* in your life.

This second nature issue is clutching to life's drama as a "normal" way of living. It invades your life in multiple ways, damages your love life, and is so ingrained in your approach to life that you may be wondering if the types of drama or their source have anything to do with you.

Why You Need to Know About Drama

Drama Queen tendencies are a version of *living by default* and are an emotional driver for the decisions you make… *usually the bad ones*.

In your love life, *Drama Queen* issues mean no good man will ever really stand a chance. He's too "normal," has his act together and wants to treat you well. Not enough drama for someone who thrives on having something to complain about, lives for the thrill of chaos, or is so comfortable with turmoil she doesn't know another way to live.

Some of you are thinking good (translation: nice) men are boring and some of you are thinking you want a good man so *Drama Queen* tendencies don't apply to you. Oh contraire on both accounts. Nice has nothing to do with boring. In fact, nice men can also have an ornery streak. Just enough so he's a little mysterious, yet not enough that he's a jerk. It's all in how you look at it.

If you are thinking you want a good man, and have every intention of giving him a chance, you may conclude this drama stuff doesn't apply to you. Dig a little deeper. *Wanting* a good man doesn't mean you've done the work on yourself to actually *choose* one.

Unfortunately, most of us have some *Drama Queen* tendencies. I suspect one of the types may ring a bell for you, plus your real friends may be able to give you some more perspective. Before we address the types, let's explore the source of the drama.

The Drama Source

The drama you seek is actually driven by emotional turmoil *inside of you*. This need for drama fuels your reaction to "life is difficult" or "life is hard" events and may even mean you stir up trouble just to get a drama fix. When things happen, *Drama Queen* reactions are much more extreme than what may really be required to resolve, cope with, embrace or celebrate a situation. Everything is better than it really is, or worse than it really is.

With dating, it probably means you seek out the men who are full of drama, either by their own character (or more likely lack of it) or how they live their life. You're probably not doing this with much conscious awareness. It's so programmed within you, its likely coming from an unconscious place and creating your life by default. Remember that means you're just running on auto-pilot, without much regard for your choices or being in charge of your own life.

Probably the best way to explain your drama source and its *damaging impact* is first understanding how you got this way, then going through the types of drama. The types are examples of the drama source in action, and the result.

You Don't Know Any Different

A key question about how you got this way – Do you know you are a *Drama Queen*, or do you just sit on your clueless throne while all your friends know this about you? Ok, maybe that's a little harsh, though I want to get your attention. Reading through this chapter may help you figure out your *Drama Queen* tendencies if you don't know them already.

Have you taken any steps to do anything different? If not, maybe it's because you don't know what to do. Or it's because this is how you grew up and it's all you know given your family or friends operate this way.

Taking this need for life mayhem and something to worry about into your love life equals "bad boys" and *B.A.T.s* all over the place. This is where "nice guys finish last" lives and dies. Well, the nice ones who have their act together are never invited into your drama world since they don't fuel your need for chaos.

That's the problem - *Drama Queen* is a comfort zone for you. It's the only way you know life to be and is why you end up in the same situations - dating the same type of men and getting the same bad results. The *B.A.T. Signs* chapter may illuminate several familiar scenarios for you. Only you can decide to change things.

Drama Types

There are several drama types that kick your internal turmoil into action: *He's All I Can Get, Ms. Fix It, The Chip on Your Shoulder, Stirring Things Up,* and *Your Baggage is Showing.*

He's All I Can Get

A huge issue is compensating for what you believe are your shortcomings and choosing icky men because you think that's all you deserve. This drama is anchored in the belief no decent man would want you. If this is your version of drama, your low self esteem is driving, not you. It speaks to you so loudly you can't hear anything else and your belief you are a good woman who deserves a good man is erased... if it ever existed. You're supposed to raise your low self esteem, not let it run your life. Note: a *He's All I Can Get Drama Queen* is an easy target for a *MEGA B.A.T.*.

There isn't an overnight solution to solving your insecurity and low self worth. It probably took several years for you to beat down your opinion of yourself so don't expect an overnight change. It *will change* as you take stock of your life, your decisions and how you want to proceed this time. A note from your *real friends*: You absolutely deserve someone decent or even better – a good man. As I said before, need to start with you first.

Being Ms. Fix It

The next type of dating drama is choosing men who have lots of drama and you want to fix it for him. You want to soothe him. Or baby him. It makes you feel needed. It's a nurturing thing on steroids. Some may call it "people pleaser." Don't mistake feeling needed by him with being loved for who you are. It's not the same.

Given he's wrapped up with his own issues and concerns, he does nothing to maintain the relationship with you because he's always needed elsewhere – at work, with his buddies, or anywhere other than helping you or being there when you need him. You become resentful as you realize you trained him not to do anything for you by always doing everything yourself, and the relationship either blows up or you sleep in separate bedrooms the rest of your life.

If you're in this situation, for your sake and his, I hope it ends. Yes, even if you have kids. Being married or involved with someone you don't want to be involved with is emotionally draining and devastating to your life in multiple ways. And, the kids know their parents aren't happy. What kind of drama example are you setting for them?

Find a different way to meet your need of being appreciated. Resolution may be a conversation with him about your needs, or it could mean making life changes and ending a relationship. Or, it could mean you'll choose differently this time because you are aware of your *Ms. Fix It* tendencies. Note: *Mr. Project B.A.T.* is catnip for *Ms. Fix It Drama Queen*. Don't skip over *The Secret – It Starts with You* chapter. It could shift your perspective altogether.

The Chip on Your Shoulder

Another type of drama is the bitter, jaded attitude many women carry around with them everywhere they go. If this sounds like you, this attitude builds a chip on your shoulder - just daring a man to knock it off and prove himself. It's like saying "I dare you to prove you are good enough for me." Who do you think you'll attract with a sneer on your face? Jerks who want to conquer, but probably won't stick around, is who.

With an extremely jaded attitude, you not only have a chip on your shoulder, you have built a wall around you. So, you're basically asking men to bring a sledge hammer, and fight through the wall. Or, more likely, it's a dare for him to see if he could knock down the wall. This is really attractive for jerks who want to wield their strength and power, and take on the competitive challenge just to see if they can do it. Sounds like fodder for a bet with his buddies. Of course, collecting the prize is on their mind too. Doesn't mean they view the prize as something they keep. Could be a catch and release thing.

So, if you are walking around oozing the energy that every man must *prove* he's worth a moment of your time, they'll sense it and the good ones will keep walking. There's a big difference between being confident and being an angry, jaded woman fearful of being hurt again. The good men know the difference and even though you are a good woman, your bitter attitude isn't conveying that.

If you insist on being stuck in this state of mind, you'll always be fearful and never enjoy the love you seek. Best to knock off the chip yourself and realize you're creating your own drama.

Stirring Things Up

Then there's the drama from the little things, like he forgot to pick up the milk – AGAIN! Yes those things can be irritating, but do they really command a melt down? Or, he finally has a job he likes and you're hell bent on getting him to change it… again! He's happy now and the drama in your life is reduced which means you're bored.

A quiet day doesn't mean things are too still and you should be sitting on the edge of your seat just waiting for the next bad thing to happen. Don't create chaos out of sheer boredom or for fear he'll leave you since there's nothing going on where he has to prove he still cares. This drama means you keep things stirred up so he has to continue to do something for you to reassure you he'll stay. Careful, he may leave you because of the drama you are stirring up for no reason other than your own insecurity, and the constant stress you bring to his life.

Are you shaking your head? "I'd never do that. I don't pick fights with him just because I'm bored or don't have anything better to do. Or I'm scared if we get too comfy or it's too easy – it means something is wrong and I need him to keep proving he loves me." That's about you, not him. Time to dig into yourself and make different choices about how you feel about yourself and how you run your life.

Your Baggage is Showing

I've heard stories from some women who know they have issues with manipulation, keep lots of secrets or are generally bitchy. The ironic part is they are seeking a man who will "call them on their crap (aka drama)." To this I say – have less drama for them to call you on. The drama solution starts with you.

If part of your list for the man you seek is he can call you on your overly emotional drama generated by hanging on to life baggage – have fewer issues to handle! Otherwise, having this on your list basically says "I'm looking for a man who will and can manage me, instead of knowing and working on myself enough I have less to manage and can manage myself." You will continue to repel the well rounded, intelligent, emotionally mature man you seek and attract the needy men who want to "fix you" yet may keep you broken so they can feel "needed." It's a sick cycle.

Some of you may read that paragraph and think – "Wow! These women sound really screwed up!" Careful not to dismiss this stuff as someone else's problem. Everyone has baggage and everyone has issues. It's what you've done and are doing about them that matters. For men and women.

A Journal Moment

If you ask yourself some tough questions and get an auto-pilot answer... you aren't digging deep enough. Be more introspective. Take some time to really consider the answer, or ask a real friend to listen to you process it out loud. They can help reflect back what you are saying and help you understand yourself. A few questions to help you get started:

- In your last relationship, what were you excited about and what did you like?

- What did you dread and what did you worry about?

- What did you know to be true? Good or bad.

- As you read through the different types of drama, which ones could you relate to and why?

Read through your answers. Notice what is about you and what is about him. If all your answers are about him, go through the questions again. Relationships involve two people so you are part of the answers too. If all your answers are about you, consider the man you were with and add some notes about him. Note what you learned about your *Drama Queen* tendencies and how you'll proceed differently this time.

What's The Alternative?

If you need challenges in your life, decide to get them from a different area than your love life. And, *learn the difference* between seeking drama in your relationships or family versus other areas of your life. To get your excitement fix - change your job, go back to school, volunteer for your favorite cause, or travel the world. Any of these are a better investment of a need for "drama," hopefully now translated into "positive challenges," than in your love life.

Understand your own drama source, drama type(s) and do something to change it. *The more you drag all the baggage from your past into the present, and hang on to your insecurity about your own value, the less likely you'll ever find your future.* The change starts with you.

What Will You Choose?

Default	Deliberate
‣ Decide *Drama Queen* is every other woman's problem, not yours.	‣ Be brutally honest with yourself about your *Drama Queen* tendencies.
‣ Refuse to explore your own drama tendencies.	‣ Ask your real friends for their perspective.
‣ Blame others for your drama.	‣ Accept your role in past choices and decide you can change.

This Time

Use these affirming statements as encouragement when you need it or to celebrate deliberate changes you're making *this time.*

- *I'm beginning to understand my own drama tendencies and vow to live differently.*

- *Drama no longer drives my choices, I do.*

- *I will continue to learn about myself and reflect upon my past so I can make better decisions in the present.*

CHAPTER 5

The Secret - It Starts with You

A common belief about the problems in dating and relationships is there are no good men left. The good ones are taken, married or gay. And the rest are scum. And, in reality, there are some who are scum. (Actually, I used a stronger word than that, but decided not to put it in print.)

Here's another reality - the common denominator for the dating problems or dating success in your life is *you*. That's either great news or terrible news - depending upon how you look at it. It's great news if you recognize the connection that you being the problem also means you are the solution. It's terrible news if you are stuck in the mindset of everyone else is the problem and you haven't taken ownership of the choices you've made in your life. If you are just starting down the dating path and already know you are the common denominator, give yourself permission to continue down that road despite the others around you who may try to convince you otherwise.

The secret to successful relationships is: It all starts with you.

Where Are You Today?

Let's start with where you are today in dating and relationships.

Returning Beginner

Maybe you're a returning beginner – meaning you are mid-life and relearning the steps to the dating dance. If you already know some improvements you'd make in yourself this time around, you're off to a great start. If you don't know what you'd do differently, this is a perfect time to discover yourself.

No, I'm not talking about your weight, your hair or your wardrobe. Changes to the outside can make you feel better, and certainly help with confidence, but more importantly - *it's the changes to the inside that make the outside glow.*

Beginner - Beginner

Maybe you are a beginner - beginner with very little experience in dating. Understanding yourself first isn't a common approach to dating or relationships. Just look at how long the line is at the men-are-scum bar where some of your friends are probably drowning their sorrows. My guess is they are only defining dating based on who he is or should be without bothering to look at themselves first. And, despite the fact it isn't working the way they want, they continue to do it anyway.

As for you - Step out of the line and into yourself. The friends who refuse to join you can be fun, though they may not be the real friends who want to grow with you.

Already Dating

If you're already dating, yet continue to focus on who he should be or what he should do or have... Stop. Stop thinking about him and starting thinking about *who you are. Defining him first only says you're willing to look at what's around you, not what's within you.*

You Want to Start with Learning About Yourself

If you're already thinking you want to learn about yourself first, then define some standards for choosing him, and have the courage to use them... now you're on a roll! The secret of starting with yourself could prevent some mistakes, pain and heartbreak, and most importantly teach you to make deliberate decisions that are good for you.

A Journal Moment

Ask yourself - *why* you are interested in dating or a relationship? What do you want to create in your life as a result?

Might be you don't know yet. That's ok. And, it's ok to be a beginner and admit it. Some men will be relieved because they are also beginners. Yes, there may be some who scoff at you for being inexperienced in dating and choose to move on. It's ok. He isn't the one you want to spend time with anyway so watch out for trying to become something he would've "wanted." That's your pride, ego and lack of experience talking. He's simply in a different place in the process than you - accept it. Own where you are, what you know, and enjoy learning along the way.

If you are more experienced in dating, still ask yourself the question and really consider the answer. Success starts with learning about yourself, knowing what you want, and *why* you want it. Your answers may shift as you continue to learn.

The Default Dating Cycle

If you are already dating – This may sound familiar.
If you haven't started dating yet – Let's break the cycle.

The Cycle Begins: *I'm FREE!!! OR I'm HURT!!!*

I'm Free: This is the part where you got out of something that wasn't working, or maybe you shouldn't have been part of in the first place.

I'm Hurt: The opposite of *I'm Free* given it wasn't your idea. You're single and don't want to be. Even if you weren't happy in the relationship that just ended, you didn't want it to end because now you are alone. (That's serious settling by the way.)

Then: *Let's have some FUN!!!*

After you've healed from the devastation of being hurt, or start celebrating being free, it's all about having fun. Your focus becomes your freedom; what you can do now that you couldn't before, running around, never staying home and thrilled this is your life.

Next: *Guess I'll Date*

You decide it would be nice to have someone to share the fun with. So, you try dating and learn it's not what it "used to be" or "didn't work like it did the last time." Your decisions are all about him, what he should be like and who you want him to be. You think about and design Mr. Absolutely Perfect (not Mr. Right for You). It doesn't work out so you decide all men are jerks, there just aren't any good ones left, or it just isn't worth the effort.

Try Again

Yep, I was right. Where are the good ones???

Try Again

Crap!!! Right again! Why does it have to be so hard???

Repeat ... Repeat... Repeat.... You're *STUCK*.

You'll stay stuck until you break the Default Dating Cycle.

The Breakthrough Epiphany

Your past starts to weigh on your mind and you find yourself thinking about what's happened before. Hmmmmm.... an epiphany hits you... maybe there are some things *I* need to work on. I *am* the common denominator of what I want, what I choose and who I choose to have in my life. Now what do I do?

You Have a Decision To Make

You're on the brink of breaking the *Default Dating Cycle*.

If you've been dating and it isn't working you could go backwards, live by default, keep repeating and doing what you've always done and still get the same poor results. Or, put your *Breakthrough Epiphany* into action and get ready for deliberate change.

If you haven't started dating yet – you have the advantage of learning from your epiphany moment about your past relationships, potentially skipping all the other parts of the *Default Dating Cycle*, and moving right into deliberate discovery.

Deliberate Discovery

After the epiphany moment you might find yourself exhaling - it's the release that says "I'm *choosing* to do things differently." Or, you might be thinking while you squirm in your chair, "Um... This is unfamiliar territory and it feels uncomfortable."

Either way - this is the moment where you start to have real *personal power*. You recognize you've made some mistakes, have done some good things, and start accepting your role in how things have turned out. It's not necessarily an easy process, and it certainly takes deliberate effort to heal.

Once you have the desire to own your past and accept responsibility for your decisions – *your life will never be the same.* You'll learn about you, who you are, who you want to become, and what you want. And it will translate into a man who is truly worthy of becoming part of your life.

You're Single, Not Alone

Being single doesn't mean you are alone. It simply means you aren't married. You still have friends, family, neighbors, pets, and colleagues at work. There is love all around you so soak it up!

The Trap

Careful of the trap where you've tried… and tried… yet nothing is working. You're so afraid you'll be single (which feels like alone in the still-single-trap) the rest of your life you do one of two things. One, you accept every man who appears to be interested, and even those who really aren't, because you *don't know the difference.* This means you've probably dated every kind of *B.A.T.* there is, plus maybe a few I didn't include in this book, all because you have no standards or are afraid to use them. Or two, no man is a possibility for you because your standards are so high and so unrealistic no one could ever measure up.

No Standards

Having no standards says you'll take what you can get instead of believing you deserve someone great. Not knowing the difference between if he's interested and if he isn't says you aren't paying attention to how he's treating you. So, you "gratefully" allow and accept whatever scraps of attention he throws your way.

Unrealistic Standards

Having unrealistic standards means you're so afraid of getting hurt he must be a genius combined with a supermodel for you to even notice him. You've decided you'll never compromise on anything ever again, have listed every possible positive attribute known to humankind and are determined he must possess them all. Instead of the list being a set of standards, it becomes a set of barriers and keeps anyone with potential out of your life.

This means you'll never date anyone, or have a relationship, since you've created a perfection list and that man doesn't exist. No one is perfect, including you, so why do you expect to find a man who is?

Take the Time

Having no standards, or having standards that are too high, also means you haven't taken the time to consider what's actually important to you and *why*. Once you've reflected on your own values, what you enjoy and how you live your life, it's much easier to assess what you want from a relationship, what you would compromise on, and *choose* someone worthy of you.

Discovering who you are takes some digging into your values, priorities and needs. One of the most important questions you can ask yourself as you learn about you is *"Why* is that important?" Keep in mind - this is an evolution not a revolution. Learning about yourself, and creating yourself, is a life long process though at its core it's about believing in your own value – according to you – not according to anyone else. This discovery is you learning about you, not about you comparing yourself to other people, nor letting them establish your value for you.

You choose what you think you deserve, so if you don't believe in you yet, you are likely choosing and putting up with idiots because you do not think you deserve any better… or even *recognize better actually exists*. Discovering what's important to you in a relationship begins with you, not with him.

A Journal Moment

- How did the *Default Dating Cycle* resonate with you?

- Which one are you - No standards, unrealistic standards or I don't know yet?

Consider the impact on your prior choices and past relationships, how you might learn from them, and how to use those lessons this time.

The Girl and Woman Within

We've all absorbed information about dating, men, sex and relationships through childhood, teen and young adult years. Combined with our adult experiences and observations of those around us, we developed a set of beliefs. Many times, this is something we picked up subconsciously, and unless you take time to reflect on your past relationships, you may not even realize what you believe or how it's translated into your decisions.

There's a big difference between a *girl* answering the question, "What do I want?" and a *woman* answering the same question. The *girl* in you may be more romantic, less aware of herself, not experienced with dating, and more focused on meeting the expectations of those around you. *Girl* priorities may be his physical appearance, what car he drives and where he lives. The *woman* answer may be more mature and focused on his character, values, and how he lives his life.

Of course, the ideal man generally combines both perspectives though the *girl* answers are based on what you think you want or what others want for you, while the *woman* in you knows yourself well enough to believe in the great relationship you deserve with the good man you seek.

Men Have a Name for It

There's even a male term for this conflicted girl/woman state of mind, B.I.T.C.H., "Babe In Total Conflict with Herself." (I don't know its origin though have heard this term from several men.) That acronym screams a woman who acts like a girl, yet is supposed to be and wants to be a woman. She's someone who says she wants a man with good values yet chooses men without any. Or, a woman who becomes someone she thinks a man wants, instead of being who she is. If she doesn't know who she is, she needs to take the time to find out.

Be with a man because you like him, not because you want him to like you. If you've found yourself spending time with men and trying to get them to like you, it's possible you've never gotten around to liking yourself let alone knowing yourself. Now you may be thinking, "I don't do that Deb!" Some of you probably don't, though those of you who reacted the strongest are probably doing it to some degree. It means you have some digging to do to uncover why you do this to yourself. I suspect part of this is your inner *Drama Queen* showing.

You may have heard this before - If you don't like you, then you probably don't respect you either which means it's not likely you're behaving in a way others will respect. As you progress though the dating process, your dating maturity will change, and you'll become more comfortable with sticking to what you want… without waffling between the girl and the woman inside you.

Bitter or Better

Divorce or a bad breakup can change your perspective for the *better* because you've taken time to learn something, or for the *bitter* because you haven't learned anything from the experience, nor examined or accepted your role in the demise of the relationship. You're behaving in this conflicted state of girl versus woman and can't figure out how to heal or what you really want. Regardless of why it's over, be happy it's done and you can move on to someone who will appreciate you and all the gifts you bring. No, I'm not talking about your talents in baking or even in the bedroom – I'm talking about his appreciation of your intelligence, values and spirit.

A Journal Moment

Think about when you were a young girl, pre-teen, and teenager. Reflect on your life lessons and decisions regarding relationships – either by your own experience, your parents, your friends, your neighbors or other people you value in your life. What messages did you receive, indirectly, directly, verbally, non-verbally, and by example?

These lessons could be by conversation, or most likely observation. What were the silent messages you received, but hadn't really realized yet? Be sure you are giving your own answer to the questions, and not what you think you are expected to answer or what might be an "appropriate" answer. Be brutally honest with yourself. These journal moments are only for you, not for anyone else to see, so tell it like it is.

Next...

Consider the *emotion* at the *root of the decisions* you've made in dating and relationships – fear of rejection, being accepted, need for validation, fear of being alone, uncertain of change, another one? Sometimes talking this stuff out with a real friend, coach or therapist can help you uncover the emotional connections.

Be the Leading Lady

Be the *Leading Lady* in your own life and expect the best from yourself and from others. Learning about you and starting with you isn't about having a goal to become a perfect person, or the perfect woman. NO. *It's about becoming the best version of yourself.* Everyone is a work in progress, regardless of how together they appear. We all have things to work on, improve and discover. The people I worry about the most are those who are so blind to their own issues they don't think they have any.

Healing from the Past – Emotional Clutter

Healing from the hurts of your life is important for your overall well being, not just your love life, and is a crucial part of becoming a *Leading Lady.* We all have emotional clutter though some appear to keep a tidy house and others look like hoarders. *Here's the difference - intellectually knowing you've made poor choices is totally different than taking ownership of those decisions and recognizing they were yours to make.* Cleaning up your emotional clutter starts with owning your decisions.

You'll never forgive yourself until you can own the fact you made the decision, get comfortable with what happened, and recognize it's in the past. This is a HUGE step toward healing whatever past baggage you are carrying around and likely dragging into the present. And, it may even be projecting into your future.

This stuff impacts far more pieces of your life than your love life. You could be hanging on to business decisions, career path choices, stuff with your kids, guilt about your parents, and uncertainty about your finances. Start today. Learn about what's holding you back, what you're holding onto, and let it go. *If you own your part of it, it can't own you.*

Consider your life – what area of your life do you most fear someone will ask you about? It's probably the most guilt ridden issue you are hiding from and the first one someone else will pick up on. Start there, own your choices and decide if you'll do things differently this time.

Know how to recognize the difference between when you are doing things to heal versus when you are hiding. It can be hard to understand the difference which is why I suggest you get help from a therapist, coach or real friend. You want him to have worked on these things so you need to also. It starts with you.

Time to let yourself off the hook for what's already done and get deliberate about making things better *this time*.

Cheating

Cheating is its own special category of emotional clutter. Those of you who were cheated on may be thinking there's an exception for you about examining your role, accepting responsibility or taking any ownership. He made the decision to cheat. Absolutely true. Whatever was going on in the relationship, he alone made the choice to respond in that manner. You decide if there's a shot at repairing the relationship based on your role, what you want, and his cheating response. Or decide if he was a *B.A.T.* from the beginning and not worthy of another chance.

If it's over, be done and value yourself enough to move on. Living your life as the "walking wounded" - always hurt or always angry - is no way to exist. Being stuck in the past or avoiding the past is certainly an indication it's time to get some professional help.

If you are the one who cheated, take very special care to understand what created the reaction in you, if you are remorseful, or if *you* are the *B.A.T.* and would do it again to someone else. Again, talking to someone may be the best way to help you sort it out.

Compromising Yourself

It's hard to be a *Leading Lady* if you are compromising yourself. For example, in many career roles, people morph to become something the company wants instead of being authentically who they are. You work to *keep* your job instead of working at a job you enjoy. I've lived it and have seen it happen repeatedly – even to the owners of the business. Sometimes it's necessary for financial reasons, or to keep the employment benefits, or for your kids. And, sometimes those are just excuses to avoid making tough choices and causing change in your life.

You Lose Yourself

Losing yourself is a sad situation and it happens in personal relationships too. All of the sudden you've lost who you are, what you value and what brings you joy in the interest of becoming part of a relationship and "supportive" of your partner. Yes, a successful relationship includes compromise - though be careful - the key is what you compromise about.

If you compromise too much of yourself, this kind of unconscious default living leads only to heartache or a mediocre life given there will be a day when you wake up and say – "HEY! I'm not happy. Now what am I going to do???"

You're Not Happy

When you're unhappy at work, you can quit your job and find a new role to suit your life. Even if you own the company, you can decide to sell it or change your role. A career transition isn't easy, though I'm sure some of you have already done it at some point. Those of you who are just starting out in your work life – be deliberate about how you proceed. Start with what you want and adjust to reality from there. No shame in making choices to suit you right now in your work life while moving toward what you want your career to become. Maybe some of your careers are leading and caring for your family. As a single woman, now is your chance to shine for yourself and include choices for you.

Just like with your work, if you're unhappy in your love life you can make changes. The problem comes if you've already chosen someone who doesn't meet your standards and now you're committed or married to him. Could you breakup or get divorced? Of course, though why not take the time to choose better in the first place. Is that a guarantee everything will come up roses? Nope. It does mean you're living like a *Leading Lady* given you chose him with your eyes wide open using your head and your heart.

Smart Women's Pride

Smart women don't want to admit they are dating an idiot. Your pride's talking, and your ego is driving the conversation. I know smart women who hide their husbands from the rest of their life because they are embarrassed by him. Is this the relationship you want? Choose better. Experience helps, and as you date you'll learn more about yourself and what you're looking for so this time you'll make more informed choices.

If You Let Your Issues Decide

If you are on a path that compromises you, who you choose to date and who you are attracted to can become a function of your own issues. If you are fundamentally insecure about your body, you'll focus on men who will see your physique as attractive. If you are uncertain about deserving love, you'll choose someone who acts as if he can fulfill that for you.

It doesn't mean this is the man who is worthy of the attractive, wonderful, intelligent woman you really are. It just means instead of doing some work on yourself first, you unknowingly seek out men who are a reflection of what's broken about you. He'll satisfy a particular issue instead of partnering with the whole you.

Break the Pattern

You won't become a *Leading Lady* unless you stop compromising yourself and make relationship decisions that truly reflect all the love and devotion you deserve.

What Does it Take to *Keep You*?

Think of dating choices this way... what does it take to *keep you* instead of *get him*? Many women I've met mold themselves into something to try and *keep him* - like they are talking him into being interested. Your low self esteem is showing if you can relate to this.

Please accept this gentle nudge – even if you have your life together otherwise, like your career or business is on track (whatever that means to you), you have good friends, family, a place to live and some money in the bank - it doesn't matter. It's hazardous if your love life continues to be patterned around what it takes to get (or keep) a boy's (man's) attention instead of what it takes for him to *deserve yours.*

Careful of The *Walk on Water* Attitude

If you find yourself with the "I'm so incredible he's gonna have to walk on water to get me!" attitude, be careful. Confidence and believing in yourself is absolutely crucial to success in life as well as relationships, personal or professional. You can overdo it and repel what you want instead of attract it.

The difference is how scared you are of being hurt again and the resulting energy you exude. When you're truly confident and approachable, you convey an "air" about you of centered and sincere. Over doing your "I'm the cat's meow of women" attitude says "I'm better than everyone else and I dare you to prove otherwise." That's fear talking, not confidence. Sometimes it's a subtle difference, though men will pick up on it.

It's the same reaction you'd have to him actually. If he's arrogant and full of himself, you may be repelled. (If you aren't, your inner *Drama Queen* may be talking, so be aware). On the other hand, if he's calmly confident and easy to talk to, you are drawn in like a moth to a flame.

Don't Be a *Doormat*

The opposite of the *walk on water* attitude is feeling so invisible you let men (and maybe women) walk all over you. You don't assert your own presence, share an opinion or believe your life could be any different. The idea of "what it takes to keep you" is a little baffling since you're always worried about people liking you. The notion of dating standards totally escapes you because you cannot imagine excluding anyone from your life, or making the tough choices to do so.

If you can relate to this, the concept of *what it takes to keep you* probably feels pretty foreign, though I suspect it's what you truly desire from a man. I also suspect you allow men in your life who have no interest in keeping you because you lack the courage to choose otherwise. Here's another gentle nudge - Get comfortable with the idea that not all men deserve a chance with you and there are some who do.

A Journal Moment

As you consider whether or not you are being a *Leading Lady*, think about what your questions are at this stage of your life and what do you want to improve about your relationships?

‣ What emotional clutter are you hanging onto?

‣ Do you catch yourself with the "walk on water" attitude?

‣ Do you have "doormat" tendencies?

‣ How did your answers impact your last relationship(s) and/ or dating choices?

‣ Are you compromising yourself? What could you do to change it?

‣ What does it take to *keep you*?

You'll Find Him When You Stop Looking

The reason for the phrase "you'll find him when you stop looking" is you stop worrying about the past, learn about yourself, live in the present and get comfortable with who you are. You can't live in the future so if you're always focused on finding a man so you can have a future, you aren't living in the present either. And you're certainly not enjoying today. Be happy with yourself and your life as a single person. Because you are single until you're not.

Expecting a relationship to make you happy instead of being happy in your life is a BIG DEAL. Being happy with yourself is the true secret to a meaningful relationship and making choices that are good for you. As a relationship evolves, you get him involved with your life and vice versa. It's a natural progression for each of you to want to do things together and care about the other's well being. It starts with YOU being involved with your life, healing from your past pain, and choosing to be who you are and how you want to grow in this life. Remember it's discovering who *you* are and what you want, not what other people think.

Sometimes we know exactly what we want. We just don't want to admit it because it's not the path we're on now and we're scared of making a change to create the possibility. Same goes for *knowing* what we deserve and *believing* in what we deserve. Knowing comes from your intelligence and believing comes from your heart. You can intellectually understand something yet still not believe it in your soul. Pushing the comfort zones of the "old you" is scary, though discovering new dimensions to yourself and what you want in a relationship, followed by believing you can have it, creates a whole new comfort zone.

Fundamentally, *you'll find him when you stop looking* is about a change in your emotional state. If you've been dating, and it was before you worked on yourself, you may have looked for him from a place of emotional desperation, not wanting to be alone, and continuing to choose men who are B.A.T.s.

After working on yourself, your emotional state becomes "I'm open to the possibilities because I'm happy with myself and I'm ready to share myself and my life with someone." That's a much more attractive state of being and interests a good man you would actually want in your life. Of course, some effort is needed to be open to the possibilities, and choose to do things you enjoy so there are opportunities to meet people where he could be "found."

The "Go Away! -- Hey Where'd He Go?" Stage

As you go through the dating process, especially if you've just left a relationship, be aware of your own healing. You may discover someone who interests you, gives you a chance to practice dating and learn more about yourself. One of the things that could happen as you heal from a bad breakup or divorce is the desire to still have someone in your life combined with the rooted fear it won't work out and you'll be hurt… again.

If you continue to date this man who interests you, and you interest him, but you haven't worked on yourself yet, you may start to feel smothered. Especially if he's attentive which I suspect your last man was not. You'll start to think you don't need him, don't want this, and wish he'd "go away" and stop bothering you. And, you put up your guarded walls even higher and sturdier. Of course, if he's not a stalking freak you should dump anyway, he'll get the hint and back off. Which will lead to you wonder "Hey! Where'd he go?"

This is the "babe-in-total-conflict-with-herself" stuff I was talking about earlier. You say you want someone in your life, yet behave as if you don't. You cover your head with the protective shield you built and hide underneath. Suddenly your schedule is too full with your job, or your kids or something. Except it's actually fear talking.

Allow time to heal from your own issues and take down the shield. Doesn't mean you have to date, or even have a desire to date. There's absolutely nothing wrong with being single and not dating. The difference is without the shield you're living as you. With the shield, you're hiding from yourself and from your life… and from any potential relationship. Then you wonder why you're single.

A divorced woman came to me with this story. Her husband divorced her after four kids and 24 years of marriage. The divorce wasn't a knock down drag out fight, though it certainly wasn't pleasant. After a while, she decided she wanted to date and test the waters a little. Well, she actually met a good man, first time out. It freaked her out so much she ran him off with her passive aggressive B.I.T.C.H. behavior, a classic version of the men's term "babe-in-total-conflict-with-herself."

See, she hadn't taken any time to heal from the past. So, this good man took the brunt of her emotional damage. To his credit, he was actually helpful to her, yet at the end of the day she treated him like dirt. Also to his credit, he wouldn't take it and broke up with her. She learned an important lesson that she needed to examine her past decisions, own her role in the demise of her marriage, and to heal her own heart before she was really ready to let someone else in.

Personal Power

When you've healed your past baggage and truly live from your own power, your life changes. Being a good person and stepping into your own power isn't about control or manipulation or being a commander. It's about *trusting yourself,* your decisions, and your instincts, and understanding that taking charge of your life creates its own reward.

You'll feel confident, capable and centered with a deep belief in your own value. You'll move through life knowing you can handle whatever comes your way, even the awful stuff. Doesn't mean you won't feel hurt, pain, anger or frustration… it means you know at the very core of your being you can survive and thrive in this life and deliberately focus on joy, gratitude and your own success… whatever success means for you.

Don't Shrink

Don't shrink from your success, so *he* feels bigger and more secure with himself. It's not your job to make him feel less insecure. It's *his* job to be secure with himself. *Your* job is to be your fantastic self and choose a man who wants you to grow into your potential and reach your dreams. He should be cheering for you to become more of yourself, versus whining about you advancing your education, getting promoted, or something else that threatens him. Of course, you should be cheering for him too. It's always a two way street.

Choices

Standing in your own power is recognizing you always have choices and feel like you are guiding your life. Notice I didn't say *controlling* your life. There are always things that happen we can't control. The need to control your life is based in fear and being uncomfortable with the unknown. Actually, a lack of personal power is usually centered in fear. Fear about direction, your path, your emotions, are you doing the right things with your life, or are you making good decisions for yourself. When you stand in your own power, you believe you have choices, even if you don't like the options presented.

Stand Up for Yourself

Living in your own power also means you are standing up for yourself and living your life according to your own standards. It brings an enormous sense of inner peace when you recognize and embrace it. This sense of calm evolves over time instead of a lightening bolt moment. Actually, a lightening bolt moment could be the trigger where you recognize the need, though establishing and living with your own sense of personal power is best when it evolves. Just like eating well – it's best if you do it each day so it becomes ingrained in your lifestyle and belief system.

Here's an example: If your head is buried so far in the sand you've been mistreated numerous times by the same man, or same type of man, and you're still not paying attention to the fact he is NOT a good choice for you... STOP. Stop everything. Stop living the way you have and make some drastic changes and I'm not talking about cutting your hair. Get away from this relationship that makes you feel small, and constantly causes you to be overly accommodating and make excuses for his idiotic behavior.

You deserve better my friend, and your *real friends* should be telling you that. In fact, they may have tried, but you are so far gone you can't hear it. Listen to yourself and how you feel about you when you are with him. Are you happy? Does he bring you joy? Do you appreciate his character and agree with his principles? Do you trust him? When he tells you something about himself or his life do you believe him? Do you feel good about you? Does he embrace you or criticize you and constantly make you become something you aren't to please him? If so, he isn't the one and he never will be. Be good to you. Stand up in your own power and make a different decision.

Power and Acceptance

As you learn about you, see yourself with forgiveness from your heart and not judgment from your head. You'll criticize yourself less, and be more forgiving of your mistakes. This attitude makes it easier for you to develop your sense of living in your own power, given perfection is not the objective. This acceptance of your own choices makes you more resistant to others' opinions potentially swaying your belief in yourself and shooting a hole in your personal power.

As you practice seeing yourself this way, try seeing others this way too. It'll help in other relationships in your life, including professional ones. You'll start to notice people respond to you differently, and you both may become more tolerant of the differences between you.

Could mean you shift the dynamics at work, with your family, your kids, your parents or your neighbors as you realize everyone sees the world through their own filter, and so do you. Might mean you are seeing what *really is*, instead of what you *wish it were* or *assumed it was*. This version of living from your own power means you are seeing what and who is around you with a new perspective, and allows you to make better choices for yourself.

Strength, Courage, Character

Taking charge of your life gives you strength to take risks, courage to say no, and depth of character to truly believe in yourself and what you want. More importantly, it allows you to embrace yourself and receive appreciation and love from others.

If He Calls or Not

One of the most common issues I hear about is if he calls or not. We constantly obsess about this one and allow it to take too much of our energy. It's a prime example of remembering a crucial part of living in your own power - *You always have choices.*

Let's say you are dating someone, and he doesn't call when he said he would, or worse yet he stood you up. When you live in your *personal power*, you don't spend time obsessing about why he didn't call, what may have happened or what you should've done differently so he would've shown up. Instead, your emotional response is more along the lines of – "I'm moving on 'cause I'm not spending time or energy worrying. If he had extenuating circumstances and sincerely apologizes – I'll decide if he gets another chance." Notice this emotion doesn't come from a manipulative, game-playing sense of entitlement. Its source is your own comfort with yourself and the belief you deserve to be treated well.

If he calls and you want to go out with him, great! If he doesn't call and you want to go out with him, well he just weeded himself out of the pack. You get to choose your attitude about whether he calls or not. Remember you are a wonderful, beautiful woman and deserve a man who appreciates you and will take action to do something about it.

You Decide

If he calls later than he said, or on a different day than he promised, you can decide if he's forgiven or not. You can assess if he's full of it. You can determine if it matters at all. These are all things that will happen at some point during the process and are opportunities for you to determine your own direction. Just like in business, when relationships get rocky because of communication issues, you can decide if you'll continue doing business or not, and how you choose to respond to the situation at hand.

Notice I said respond not react. There's a big difference. Reacting is generally without any thought and full of emotion. Respond implies reflective, deliberate action. The time you have to reply in either case may be the same, though the personal comfort and calm feeling is very different in react versus respond.

Be Deliberate

Choosing someone to be in your corner should be made with heartfelt thought, and common sense reason. There is business to life that needs to be addressed like money, where you will live, your home, and who will do the dishes. There's also the love, joy, passion and butterflies in your stomach that comes with someone you may be interested in and are attracted to. Why on earth would you let yourself choose by default instead of being deliberate? Be purposeful about choosing a man who appreciates who you are and loves and supports you in who you want to become.

You Can't Avoid the Risk… Unless You Stay Single

Carefully navigate your direction during this transition process and own all of your decisions. Some may say you are "guarded" and won't let anyone get close to you. That's fear talking and it isn't pretty. Being guarded is trying to protect yourself from the risk of getting hurt again. Not possible. Getting hurt is a possibility in any relationship, unfortunately. Success is also a possibility. If you aren't willing to take the risk, you might as well decide to be single. Nothing wrong with being single, unless you don't want to be. It's self-defeating to refuse to try dating because you might get hurt. You can't have a relationship without taking a risk. It just doesn't happen.

A Measure of Success

You'll know you've succeeded at living from your own power when you can stand up and say, "If it doesn't work out, I'll be ok. If it does, I'll be thrilled!" And you actually believe it in your soul, not just saying it with your head and words. There's a HUGE difference. Remember, one is your intellect talking, and the other is your belief in yourself and trusting your ability to cope with the outcome.

Be Yourself and Have Fun

Be who you are, know yourself and what you want, and most importantly, have fun! The more experience you have in dating and relationships, the more comfortable you'll become with trusting your decisions, having faith in yourself, and embracing whatever happens.

A Journal Moment

Embracing your own *personal power* isn't a light switch. As I said, learning about yourself is an evolution not a revolution. It takes a little digging into what's important to you and why. And it requires the courage to make some changes.

- How comfortable are you with your own personal power?

- What do you like about the idea of *personal power?* What concerns you?

- What keeps you from living from your power?

- Did the scenarios mentioned in this chapter ring any bells?

- What will you do differently this time?

Read through your answers to all the questions in this chapter. What jumps out at you? Anything repeated multiple times? Anything you see as a theme or you find yourself wondering, "What was I thinking?!" Maybe there's something you see you're proud of. Doesn't mean it was easy. Might be there are things you're not so proud of. Make a list of the good decisions you made and a list of things you would do differently this time. Use these lessons to make better choices now.

Sometimes the first step in knowing yourself is realizing how little you know. Sometimes it's acknowledging what you do know. Regardless, start from wherever you are today and use what you learn this time.

What Will You Choose?

Default	Deliberate
▸ Don't need to learn about myself so I'm skipping this part.	▸ Figure out what you want from dating or a relationship and why.
▸ No need for me to change even though what I've been doing isn't working.	▸ Reflect on your past decisions, their emotional root, and how you got to today.
▸ It's everyone else's problem, not mine.	▸ Be a Leading Lady, heal from your emotional clutter, and stop compromising yourself.
▸ Decide you have no influence over your own life so what's the use in trying.	▸ Take charge of your life, live in your own power and examine what it takes to keep you.

This Time

Use these affirming statements as encouragement when you need it or to celebrate deliberate changes you're making *this time*. Say them to yourself, say them out loud, or write them down in your journal - whatever is most impactful for you to remember these promises to yourself.

▸ *I value myself enough to learn what's important to me first and then think about what I want from a man.*

‣ *Unless I'm willing to take a risk, I will continue to be single.*

‣ *I live from my own power and make deliberate decisions that are good for me.*

‣ *My ongoing objective is to become the best version of myself.*

CHAPTER 6

B.A.T.s
Signs and Types of Bad Ass Trouble

The *B.A.T.s* are the men we get sucked into, yet can't, or won't, let go of. He's trouble from the beginning and we make excuse after excuse about why he isn't where he said he'd be, lies about his life, and treats you like an afterthought. There are several *Signs* of *Bad Ass Trouble* men, and several *B.A.T. Types,* so be alert.

Is every man you meet going to show some *B.A.T. Signs* or be one of the *B.A.T. Types?* There's no way to predict. Does every man who is a *B.A.T.* know it? Some do it on purpose, some don't, and some are just clueless. Some will always be a *B.A.T.* because of their character, or more accurately lack of character, and some are *B.A.T.s* due to their circumstances so it might be temporary.

If you are attracted to *B.A.T.s,* or have chosen them in the past, its likely your real friends will be trying to tell you something and you should listen. At the end of the day – it's your choice, though if people who love you are raising their eyebrows, perhaps they are trying to save you from yourself. If you're new to dating, be aware this *B.A.T.* stuff exists and steer clear.

Learning the *B.A.T. Signs* and recognizing the *B.A.T. Types* is a part of growing and getting better at dating and relationships. Recognizing a *B.A.T. before* you allow him in your life is even better.

Signs of the Bad and Idiotic

Some things seem obvious, though believe me, we women are experts at justifying a man's behavior and letting him use us if we like him. Yikes. Here are the general *B.A.T. Signs* to look out for, followed by the *B.A.T. Types.*

No Room for Compromise

He always has the right answer, at least he thinks so. And when you try to have a reasonable conversation about something, he flatly disagrees and won't discuss it further. Talk about controlling. If he has such a high opinion of his views and isn't even open for discussion of another perspective, think about how it could translate into a life together. Yikes. Sounds like the household would be a dictatorship.

Inconsistencies

His story changes frequently. He says he's going one place, and then is somewhere else. He spends time with a few friends, except he's not actually with them. Says he needs to be at work, and then ends up on the golf course. Yes, there are days when what you plan gets totally changed and you end up doing something entirely different. That's not what I'm referring to here. This is the man who says one thing and does another. Says he is a "family" man, and shows you otherwise. Declares you are important, then leaves town for two weeks and doesn't call you. When what he says and what he does don't match, it spells trouble.

Something Doesn't Add Up

Here's where some of the obvious stuff should come in, like you're asked not to call him or you still don't know where he works. Or, he changes his story frequently yet always seems to have the "right" answer to justify his behavior... that should get your instincts peaked. Especially since we women have great intuition and it's an incredible asset if you let yourself trust it. It's that little voice saying – "What's up with this guy?"

I've heard stories like he wouldn't give out his birthday, where he grew up, or how big his family is. How strange is that? If your gut says something doesn't add up, it probably doesn't. Could be he's married. Could be he's a felon. Do you really need to hang around and find out? Yes, could be he's going through a rough time in life and you're convinced I'm being too hard on him. Just know the intrigue you're feeling may be the "bad boy" magnet getting you in trouble. I suggest opening your eyes to see the situation more clearly. Look at him with some objectivity, not the lustful "he's so HOT!" reaction you're having.

Never Met His Friends - Doesn't Want to Meet Yours

After you've dated awhile, or immediately depending upon how you met, you'll eventually meet each other's friends. Except when his are always out of town, or busy, or somehow unavailable. Could be he's hanging out with his friends and being a bachelor, knowing he has you waiting on him whenever he's ready. (Don't be the woman waiting for him to get around to you. You have a life to live.) Could be there's a connection to an ex you are unaware of.… could be he doesn't have any friends… could be he's embarrassed by them because he does value you and they are not the friends you would be impressed by. As with all the signs, be aware of the situation and make choices that are good for you.

Only Compliments Your Physical Appearance

He only talks about sex or compliments your physical appearance. You don't have discussions about intelligent topics, or ever discuss ideas. It's only about what you are wearing when you saw him last and what you'll wear when you see him next. Sounds like he's only in it for the sex. If that's what you want, and he's respectful of what you like in bed, then it's your choice to make. Just don't mistake his lust for you with loving you. Lust exists without love. And, don't kid yourself into thinking he'll suddenly develop deep-seated love for you. Most men don't need emotion to have sex.

Drinks Too Much

This one is relative to your own drinking habits, though most reasonable people agree there is a line between how much is sociable versus how much is "party-man," or worse yet, alcoholic tendencies. Don't ignore this. And, be smart about getting in the car with someone after they have been drinking. (Duh!) Choosing the one who is "less drunk" than the others is a careless excuse I've heard several times and it's still idiotic.

This is a special example of showing your *dating age* and trying to re-live your party years. Or maybe you missed your party years. Or maybe you didn't leave your party years. Be smart about your own safety both in how much you'll drink (you don't have to drink at all) with someone you don't know, or if you are riding with him and he's been drinking. This isn't the time to worry about hurting his feelings if he's not sober to drive and you rode with him. (Of course, if you are just meeting him, you shouldn't be riding with him anyway! Use your head. Would you want your daughter, sister, niece, mother or someone else you love riding with a stranger? Be smart. Meet him in a well-lit public place, don't ride with him.)

Your Friends Vanish

This sign isn't one that comes from him. It's the result of him. If your friends vanish after you started dating him, it could be because they can't stand being around him and watching you make the choice to date so far below your standards. Learn the difference between a man worthy of you and one who isn't, and listen to your real friends who have tried to have an honest conversation about it. Wake up woman! If your guy is the only one around, maybe it's time to listen to your real friends' perspective. I didn't say you have to agree with them, though something is up if your friends vanish. Find out what.

He Cheated in Prior Relationships

The fact he admits he cheated is a start. It could mean he's admitting to making a bad choice and a big mistake and is being honest with you about it. This assumes he actually feels remorseful about this horrible decision and recognizes it wasn't an appropriate way to respond to what was happening at the time. Watch for patterns where he's done this in multiple relationships, and watch for the other signs.

Inconsistencies in his story or behavior could mean he'd do it again, or already is. Don't make yourself paranoid about this one. Trust your gut. Truly listen to it. Be quiet. Turn off the TV and all other noise and ask yourself if you truly trust this man. Don't ignore it when the first answer is NO. My stance on cheating has always been – "Your crap is on the lawn."

On the flip side of this one - I truly believe people can change and evolve. If he's admitting fault, is remorseful, truly learned something, and you believe you can trust him, he may earn a chance. If he's still prone to this stupidity, it'll show up in time. Use your head - if there are too many other factors added to this one and you think something doesn't add up - it probably doesn't. Your choice if he's worthy of a chance with you.

Only Talks About Himself

In this sign, he only talks about himself, doesn't ask about you and cuts you off if you try to share something about yourself, your life or even your day. I've heard stories where the man actually told the woman he was dating not to share stories about various aspects of her life because he didn't want to hear about them. Talk about a man who is only interested in his own needs and not in yours. Next!

Says He Doesn't Know What He Wants from a Woman

Believe him and hang up the phone. Everyone has morals, values and standards - men included. Not everyone is a planner, or writes down their standards and values, that is true. However, even if they aren't written, they still exist. So, if he says he doesn't know what he wants from a woman, it most likely means he's never taken the time to learn from his past relationships, owned his mistakes and made different choices for himself. You're welcome to date him and help him learn, just know you are his tutor and he may take his new found knowledge on the road… and not with you.

Your Physical Reaction

Your stomach is always in knots and it's because he's creepy, not because he's dreamy and you're nervous. Pay attention to this. Your gut knows a lot.

Flashes Money

Many women dream of the millionaire with the good heart who will sweep them off their feet… the ultimate fairy tale of the man with the golden heart and the platinum bank account. Whatever your values are for money and how much he's supposed to have - here's my point: If he's flashing money yet has nothing to talk about, run. That's *Mr. Project B.A.T.* in disguise given his insecurity is hidden by his ability to impress you with fancy dates and stories of lavish spending. Ask yourself, does he have any depth? Is he attractive to you in any way other than his wealth? Guess if your values align with the "gold digger" stereotype where money is the only thing that matters, then you've found your man. Otherwise, the money may be nice, but the relationship won't have the depth you seek or the connection you long for.

Be careful if he's flashing money to be sure he actually has some to flash. Men can be gold diggers too so be cautious he's not fishing for your money - especially if he starts asking personal questions about your finances. Believe me, I'm a huge proponent of discussing finances in a relationship, though it's a topic for someone you are considering living with or marrying, not for someone you just met.

Only Calls at the Last Minute

He says he wants to spend time with you yet never makes any plans. He says he wants to date, yet only calls at the last minute. Then, he claims you are the problem because you're never available when he calls. Let's cut to the chase – you aren't a priority. Especially since he probably manages to see his buddies and may even plan things with them like tickets to a ballgame. You're never quite sure how he spends his time given straight answers aren't part of his make up.

A connected issue is if you do see him, and he expects sex from you. Of course, if you give it to him you are part of the problem since you're responding to the Booty Call. If you want a relationship, it's not likely Mr. Only Calls At The Last Minute will ever be a candidate for you. He's great for Mr. Casual Sex and some short-term fun – though not likely a candidate for an ongoing thing.

I'm not saying everything in the rest of your life will be planned out well in advance. I am saying when you first meet someone and are in the beginning of dating, expect him to show that you are a priority. Spontaneity or changing plans at the last minute is something you can work out in a relationship, after dating becomes one.

He Drives by the Ex's House with You in the Car

Just had to throw this one in because I heard the story directly from the woman it happened to. He even *told* her why they were taking this route, and it wasn't the most direct to the restaurant. Clearly this man isn't ready to move on. Clearly she needs to raise her standards and if she continued to date him, admit to her inner *Drama Queen.*

He Knows How to be Arrested

Here's another I heard… A friend of mine shared a story of a boyfriend. He went over to her house, got drunk and belligerent. She called the cops. When they arrived, he put his hands behind his back like he'd done it before. Yikes on getting drunk and belligerent. Double yikes given it seems he'd been arrested before.

How He Communicates

You call and he texts you back. You see him and he spends all his time texting or talking on the phone with someone else. When you aren't together, your conversations tend to happen by text or email, not voice to voice. Is it just his style, does he have poor communication skills, or is he just having a busy time at work? Could be all of those things. Could be he doesn't see you as important or important enough to make the effort to actually *talk* with you.

Don't expect him to communicate like you would; he's not you. This doesn't excuse taking you for granted or treating you like an afterthought. Learn about his communication style, pay attention to how he cares for you (or not), and how this sign mixes with any others you notice. You decide if it's an issue or not.

You should also pay attention to your own communication style and habits relative to how you treat him. Examine your own *B.A.T. Sign* on this one.

Promises The Future Way Too Soon

Could be he enjoys being in a relationship and actually likes being married. Maybe he actually knows himself well enough and has done some work on his own issues so this excitement for a future with you comes from a healthy emotional place. That's the romantic in me talking.

The flip side is he's insecure living alone, being single and can't stand his own company. You are a welcome *distraction* to his life though not necessarily someone he *wants*. Another option is he hates housework and is looking for a wife/cook/housekeeper so he doesn't have to do it anymore – or start doing it at all. No magic answer on figuring this one out though it could be related to *Mr. Project B.A.T. Type* explained below. As with all the signs, be aware and go into this with your eyes and your senses wide open and paying attention.

B.A.T. Types

B.A.T.'s come in several types. Some men are *B.A.T.s* because of their situation and some are *B.A.T.s* because of who they are, or allowed themselves to become. A situational *B.A.T.* could come out of *B.A.T.* status when their situation changes, assuming they've done the work needed to recover from their circumstances and not carry it on to you. A *B.A.T.* where it's part of their personality or character may never change and are *toxic* to you.

MEGA B.A.T. – The Ultimate Trouble

"The more you're an ass and ignore women, the more they convince themselves they can't live without you." Quote from a single man – so sad there's some truth to this statement.

The *MEGA B.A.T.* thinks he walks on water. The bigger problem is you believe him. It isn't because he's done anything terrific, or treated you with any exceptional respect. It's how he acts in general... full of ego. Some may say all "sizzle" and no "steak." He's shallow. He lacks depth. This man is playing you and getting his jollies doing it. He combines all of the signs listed above and then some. He's the ultimate "bad boy" who treats you like dirt and you keep going back for more.

He makes lots of promises he doesn't deliver on, though always appears to have a good reason. His temper may be short and you find yourself appeasing him every step of the way. You are always accommodating his schedule, dealing with his arrogance and insecurities, soothing his outbursts, and walking on eggshells so you don't set him off.

He's deceptive, manipulative, doesn't seem to have a conscience, and doesn't care or even recognize the consequences. This is a game to him, may feed his competitive nature, with zero emotional attachment. He wants to win you, not keep you. He may have flat told you he doesn't want a relationship, yet you keep going back for more torture.

His charm and good looks are hard to resist and everyone thinks you've found the perfect man. It's so easy to keep up appearances since you frequently hear you two "look so good together" and he behaves like a gentleman around other people. Yet when you're alone, you're holding on to hope and a wish that he'll change because that's all ya got.

I suspect he picked you because you are an easy target. Maybe you met him before you worked on you and realized your own power.

Or, maybe you're early in the dating process and don't have much experience yet. It doesn't matter because you still have instincts and the little annoying voice in your head saying, "What are you thinking???" On top of everything else, he may even have a tan line on his wedding ring finger you are ignoring.

If you date a *MEGA B.A.T.* – that's about you. You picked him and you keep dating him. And, most likely, on some level - you know you are doing it. Every time he mistreats you, then does something to redeem himself, you ignore all the signs he's wrong for you. Instead it's a constant fight with yourself, or crying to your girlfriends, "Why do I keep doing this to myself???" (Does the *He's All I Can Get Drama Queen* sound familiar?)

If the girlfriend you cry to doesn't try to knock some sense into you, then you need to find the *real friend* who will. The supportive one means well, but she isn't helping your dating outlook. And, you can help her get some sense if she's also dating a *MEGA B.A.T.* and she keeps saying, "It's ok. He's a man and you know how they are." That's bull. Yes, men and women are different. But WHY would you choose to spend time with the ones who are clearly jerks.

Get some standards and USE them!

Drunk B.A.T.s Can't Dance

Drunk *B.A.T.s* can't dance… They'll mess up your rhythm, and not just on the dance floor. Ok, now we're getting into some serious issues. Is he drunk a lot or is this just one night? Did you even notice or were you drunk too?

No judgment on enjoying a beverage of choice in moderation. Liquid courage can help with your nervous nerves. Though if you met him and he was drunk – did you learn anything real about him? Be careful not to think the things you learn about a drunk, horny man in a bar are true. Of course, if you were the drunk, horny woman, then maybe you were a match. At least for the night.

Be careful to be true to yourself in these situations. He's not himself if he's drunk and neither are you. The man you met isn't the real man you'll be dating if you pursue something so be sure the next time you see him – there's no alcohol involved. It'll give you a clue if he can do something social without alcohol, if you like him when he's sober, and if you like him when you're sober.

He's Not Interested

If he's not calling, or seeing you, or only calls late at night… he's not interested. If you let him come over to your house late at night, you just became the convenient *booty call*. If you're into that and this is a man with sexual skills you like, well, you make the decision. If you want a relationship, this isn't the guy who is going to give you one, and probably isn't a man who is worthy of you. If you continue with him, you're creating your own *B.A.T.* situation - his lack of initiative should tell you something. Choose to spend time with someone who is interested in you.

Vanishing Man

Unfortunately, you don't know about this *B.A.T.* until he actually vanishes. Call it his "chicken" way of breaking up with you. If he stops calling, or returning any communication from you – you just got dumped. He just didn't have the guts to say anything to you. He'll say it's because he didn't want to hurt you. That's probably true in most cases though mostly it's because he didn't want to deal with the breakup drama and all the times you're going to ask "But why???" Still, he should be an adult and have the conversation, though he won't, so stop asking.

Mr. Project

Here's the gist: he's stuck in the past, hasn't done any work to address his role in what's wrong with his life, and he's a mess. Everything is always someone else's fault, including why his past relationships ended. And, it could be he's had a lot of big events in life he's never dealt with. Or, it could be he just went through a breakup.

Most likely, he doesn't know he's a mess. However, someone fresh out of a breakup is a project because of the very nature of this emotional, life changing event. (This includes women too by the way.) Doesn't matter if you are the one who got dumped or you were doing the dumping. Unless you have no soul whatsoever, it affects you.

It's the reason the "rebound" person became a type. With a rebound man you become the person who helps him work through the pain of whatever makes him a project and help him get on with his life. *Mr. Project* is probably not malicious, or intentional about potentially hurting you. He's simply unaware of how broken he really his. And, if you are also unaware, it spells heartache most of the time since you get emotionally attached to him and he doesn't return the feelings. He's looking to fill a void; he's not necessarily looking for you.

"Fix-it" women are drawn to these men because they have so many things "to fix" and your need to be needed goes on overdrive. (*Ms. Fix It Drama Queen* may ring a bell.) Of course, lots of times once *Ms. Fix It* has restored his self esteem, he takes his new found confidence on the road.

Mr. Project also surfaces after a divorce. Same channel, same emotional turmoil as a breakup only much deeper, with bigger baggage and an ex-wife thrown in for good measure. Lots of needy, emotional stuff usually means you end up talking more about the relationship, it's status, and whether you are going to continue, than actually enjoying each other's company. Especially if you both happen to be analytical types who over examine everything. If you are the overly analytical type and he isn't, now he's drawn to you because he can learn and "get through this" while he's moving on in his life. If you are the fun one and he's the overly analytical type, he stays because you're a hoot to be around and make him laugh. Either way, you continue to stay because you feel needed.

Did I say this could never work into something serious? Nope. Though after all the hard work and feelings you have for him – is he doing the same for you or are you only someone to help him get through the rough patches? Pay attention - you know the answer. It's somewhere inside of you or it's coming from your real friends. When you ignore your gut when it's trying to tell you to move on, you are in danger of *settling*.

The thing about *Mr. Project* is his *B.A.T.* status may be temporary. How long he's a *B.A.T.* could depend upon why he's a project, if he's doing anything to address his emotional baggage and how it relates to you. However, don't let him string you along. This could take years and you have a life to live in the mean time!

To be fair here... women can be projects too. We are our own version of projects after a breakup and many other times as well. This project stuff just doesn't evaporate into thin air because you want it to. It takes effort, self awareness and the desire to change.

Just Divorced

This *B.A.T.* type is a special version of *Mr. Project*. He constantly talks about his ex-wife, or past girlfriends and all the things they did to him or against him. He bitches about what she did, or didn't do, or wish she'd done. He's constantly comparing you to her, and tells you about it. "My wife (hopefully ex-wife!) never did, let me do, liked, had or did whatever it was he thought should've happened." Seriously, why would you want to date someone who is still so hung-up on his ex that he's out with fabulous you and bitching about her? Are you his therapist? When he gets over her, then go out with him. If your first response was, "... but *he's different...*" with kind of a whiney voice and a tilt of your head, see the *B.A.T. Type Mr. Project* and get out of your *Cinderella Head*.

My rule of thumb is he needs to be divorced about a year though there's no magic formula. Some people need longer than a year to heal, some need less. It may depend on how long he was married or how engaged he was in the relationship with his ex-wife. If he's still involved in a relationship with her, you'll want to learn why. This ongoing connection may or may not be necessary, though it will impact his ability to heal. Regardless, the real question is if he's done any work on himself to take responsibility for his role in the past, let go of it, and learn something to use this time.

A year gives him time to mourn the relationship, sew his wild oats (whatever that means for him), and perhaps be ready to date and welcome someone new. If you're looking for a relationship, you don't want to be part of the sewing the wild oats phase. Nothing for you there – well maybe some sex. Ok, use a condom and be careful about convincing yourself settling for casual sex is ok with you.

Recently divorced is usually a state of mind for short-term fun, not for serious relationships. Unless, of course, he's trying to replace his ex-wife by finding a new one because fundamentally he doesn't want to be alone. Now you're just a substitute. The worst ones in this *B.A.T. Type* don't actually know themselves well enough to understand how they operate. Yikes. Watch out. He may have good intentions, though his emotional state most likely isn't stable enough to be worthy of you.

Being divorced, or worse yet – not quite divorced, doesn't make him a bad guy. It just means his emotional state, whether he knows it or not, could interfere with figuring out where he is in life, what he wants and making good decisions. Doesn't mean he's malicious or calculating, just means he doesn't know what he doesn't know. So, your job is to make good decisions for yourself, evaluate the risk, and have the strength to steer clear of this situation. Be aware of your *Drama Queen* tendencies because you may be attracted to this mixed up man so watch yourself.

Another part of the *Just Divorced B.A.T. Type* is kids. If he has children with the ex and their relationship is toxic… you've been warned. You will end up in the middle, regardless of how much you think you won't. Why would you want to put yourself in that position? Yes, it could be all her. Or, it could be all him. My experience says it's not likely a relationship could be so toxic without both people screwing it up. If you choose to proceed with dating him, remember to examine the other *B.A.T. Signs* and decide if he's worth it and more importantly, worthy of you. Again, this is prime time *Drama Queen* fuel so be aware of your *Drama Queen* tendencies.

Now you may be thinking… "I'm just divorced! So what about me?" Well, you may be a *B.A.T. Type* for him. My question is – how are you behaving? Are you always talking about your ex? Are you still fuming over your divorce and what he did or didn't do to you or for you? Have you done any healing to move past all the hurt and anger? As much as he needs to be in a healthy emotional state, you do too. It's *always* a two-way street.

Mr. Separated

It's not over till it's over. Separated isn't single - it's married. Yes, he's going through a rough time in his life, though hopefully he and his wife are working on their relationship and trying to figure out if they will make it through or end their marriage. Of course, it may depend upon why they are separated and the reasons they are having enough problems to remain in that uncertain state.

Mr. Separated B.A.T. Type could also combine some of the other *B.A.T. Types* and *B.A.T. Signs,* though he certainly is *Mr. Project B.A.T.* and could pile on *Just Divorced B.A.T.* if that's the route his marriage takes. Nothing about his complicated life spells anything good for you. Choose someone who is available to choose you.

Again, you might be thinking, "I'm separated. What about me?" Good question. Are you working on your marriage or working on your exit plan? Only you can decide if the reasons you are separated are enough to end it, or find out if you want to work through it. And, yes, you are a *B.A.T.* for the men who date you. Doesn't mean you are a bad person, assuming the men you date know you are married, it just means your life is really complicated.

Pattern Man

If you find yourself noticing more things about him that are just like your ex-husband, or ex-boyfriend, or multiple prior men in your life -- you should RUN. Have you really made any different choices for yourself or are you like I was in my early twenties; dating the same type of jerk - he just had a different name? And I wondered why I was still single – I was choosing the same kind of man, with the same characteristics and lack of values, as the one before. Rinse. Repeat. Get the same result. This *B.A.T.* isn't about attracting the wrong men, it's about *being attracted to* the wrong men.

You may need your real friends to help you recognize this *B.A.T.*. It can be tough to figure out on your own because you are in the middle of it and neck deep in all the emotions. If your friends say the same thing about everyone you're dating, wake up to the pattern. That's why the outside perspective and honesty from your real friends is important.

Mamma's Boy

This one has a triple twist. The first twist is he lives with his mother and her health is fine. Why would you want a man who still doesn't take care of himself? Yikes, this man is not looking for a partner, he's looking for a caretaker - someone to fill in where his mother left off. A good indicator is if he comes over to your house, sits on the couch and lets you wait on him without offering, or doing, anything to help. The funny part is this man will say he wants an independent woman with a mind of her own, and he probably does. The kicker is he also expects you to take care of him and the house too.

Ok, let's examine why he's still at Mom's. The exception to this *B.A.T.* is if his Mother or Father is in ill health and he is their caretaker. Then I could see living with her. Better yet, she lives with him. See the difference? It's about the choices and being independent enough to make them. The worst part is he may not know what he's expecting of you. It's unconscious behavior on his part – he's been programmed his whole life to have a woman take care of him.

Careful though, I've seen the "ill health" excuse used to cloak the fact he's just free-loading off his parents and they would be just fine on their own. Maybe they are in their senior years and a little slower than they used to be, but otherwise they are doing just fine. This *Mamma's Boy B.A.T.* is basically a teenager with means!

Here's the second twist - the Mother and Father are part of the problem. If parents have an adult son (or daughter) who has no life skills it is likely, 1. they've created their own reality in not having expectations of their children to live independently, nor have they taken time to teach their kids those skills, and 2. they allow their adult children to live in their home when there isn't really a valid reason, then 3. The parent is part of the *B.A.T. Type.* The parent is now part of keeping their adult child dependent upon them and it's not helping the situation. ("Enabling" is the word you may have heard to describe this scenario.) If the man you are considering dating is aware his mother is a control freak who tries to run his life and he doesn't allow it – that's one thing. If he's oblivious – run! He's looking for a mamma replacement.

If you are a parent who has set up this expectation - please stop. You are raising mamma's boys and mamma's girls both. Your children will grow up without the basic life skills they need to live on their own and make their own decisions. Part of your job as the parent is to help them become self sufficient, productive adults, not keep them dependent upon you. Yes, we want a man who loves his parents and cares for them and we are grateful to you for raising men who fit this description. But, not the one who is so dependent upon you he can't make any decisions without you!

Which brings me to the last twist on the *Mamma's Boy B.A.T. Sign* – Mamma has a power trip over her baby boy. That's right – he doesn't make decisions without her. About anything. There are adult relationships with our parents that are helpful, healthy and truly meaningful. And, it's a reciprocal relationship where everyone is now an adult and discussing adult issues.

The problem comes when Mamma has a power trip over Junior's life and Junior still let's her run it. She approves of his dates. Approves his diet and even makes his food. Not everyone is a talented cook or even enjoys cooking. That's not what I'm talking about. And, I'm not saying she couldn't or shouldn't have an opinion about who he dates or she can't make him a meal occasionally. However, there's a huge difference in having an opinion and expecting to make the choice for him. When it's the latter, she is still living in her adult son's life as if he never grew up. I can't say RUN loud enough here. If he's still allowing it to happen he thinks it's "normal," and I'd bet he's comparing his dates to his Mother.

For all of you who are Mother's and freaking out right now at the notion of being told how to raise your sons (or daughters), here's my comments. Intelligent, adult women want a man who appreciates and loves his mother, treats her well and respects her role in the family. Kudos to you who have raised sons who love you, like you and want to spend time with you. It's not what I was referring to in this section and I suspect you already know that.

Looks Good on Paper Man

He may be smart, educated, come from the kind of family you like, in the right geographic area, and has a stable job. That doesn't tell you what he believes, how he lives or how he'll treat you.

His resume may say he went to an ivy league college, has an "important" career, seems to be financially stable, and drives a nice car. However, it doesn't tell you if he likes his mother, is kind to his family or even speaks to them. It doesn't say if he likes being a father (if he has kids) or if he does anything to care for them. It doesn't say if he has any friends. It doesn't say what his spiritual or religious beliefs may be or how he practices them. It doesn't say how he grew up or if he's overcome some of the issues of his past.

Learning about all of those things needs to be experienced. I've been on dates with men who have a stellar resume yet have zero scruples. I suspect one particular man would've sold his dog if it advanced his career. (Thanks to my fellow pet people who are outraged at that comment.) The conversational depth only included his job. Nothing was said about his family and this particular man had kids! Nothing! Not a word about them. So, if I had only gone by his credentials, without considering what he believed or how he lived, it would have been a miserable relationship.

Of course, the reason for my potential misery is I didn't share his belief system. I guess if you are a woman who doesn't care about your family and prefers someone who doesn't speak to their children, then this man would've been great for you! Those of you who are trying to justify why he may not have talked about his kids take note of your auto-pilot need to come up with a good reason for his behavior. *Not every man deserves a chance with you so get comfortable with the idea.*

Once a B.A.T. Always a B.A.T.?

I used to think so. Then I met some men who showed me even when a man was a malicious *B.A.T.* when he was young, it is possible for him to mature and become an adult man with principles who is respectful of women (and people in general). And, recognize what a jerk he was in his younger days.

Now, don't let this be permission to hang onto the "he'll change for me" excuse and continue dating a *B.A.T.* you know in your gut is just plain trouble. I'm just saying even the nice ones at an older age may have been *B.A.T.s* when they were younger. Doesn't make them evil, just means they have actually grown up. Of course, I've heard numerous times there are plenty of *B.A.T.s* in their forties, fifties and up so pay attention to the signs!

A Journal Moment

‣ Did you catch yourself laughing or grimacing because you recognize someone you've dated? How did it turn out?

‣ Were you nodding with the *B.A.T. Signs* and *B.A.T. Types* because you've seen them before? Make a note of which ones those were and what you did about them. If you could do it again, what would you do differently?

‣ Are these all new to you? Make a note if it's because you're so new to dating, or if it's because you haven't been paying attention. This time you'll know what to watch for.

We Allow It

In some ways *B.A.T.s* exist because we women allow them to. If we didn't tolerate or justify this kind of ridiculous behavior, it might change how men act and how they treat us. When you feel weak, unworthy and broken you are most susceptible to *B.A.T.s*. It's a "shot" at having what you want, yet compromising yourself to find it. And, in the end, it's not what you truly want - especially since you're living far, far away from your own power. Sometimes that's the lonely talking. And, sometimes it's just being naive. And, sometimes it's just plain inexperience with dating and relationships.

If you're choosing *B.A.T.s* you could be seeking validation for yourself. Chasing someone who isn't interested just to see if you can catch them is a version of checking to see if you are worthy. If you continue dating *B.A.T.s*, you don't believe in you yet, nor have you learned to stand up in your own *personal power.*

You deserve the best life has to offer and that includes the love of a good man. We <u>choose</u> who gets a chance — not take what we can get.

What Will You Choose?

Default	Deliberate
‣ Deny you've ever made any mistakes dating men who may have some *B.A.T.* tendencies.	‣ Recognize not every man is nice and not every man is a *B.A.T.*.
‣ Choose to date *B.A.T.s* even though you know it isn't working.	‣ Learn the *B.A.T. Signs* and *B.A.T. Types* and pay attention.
‣ Decide you won't meet anyone this chapter applies to and ignore it.	‣ Listen to your gut and your real friends.
	‣ Have the strength to walk away.

This Time

Use these affirming statements as encouragement when you need it or to celebrate deliberate changes you're making *this time.*

‣ *I see the B.A.T.s I've dated before and will make different choices this time.*

‣　　*I know not all men are B.A.T.s, though I learn the signs of those who are and make good decisions for myself.*

‣　　*I have the courage to walk away from situations and men who aren't good for me.*

‣　　*Not every man deserves a chance with me.*

CHAPTER 7

Choosing Who Gets a Chance

There's a big difference between who you *end up with* versus *who you choose*. *End up with* implies he arrived on your door step and you lost your ability to think for yourself. Like you had no options. No, I'm not talking about the weak in the knees feeling making you tongue tied. I mean your reaction to him becomes a shrug while you're looking at the floor and act like he's the only one who showed up so he must be someone you should date. Or, you're afraid he'll be the only one who shows up. Ever.

Not Every Man Deserves a Chance

Ending up with someone is not living deliberately. It's dating by default at its finest and implies you have no needs, standards or desires so whoever shows up will do. You act like he must be a good choice though you haven't taken the time to figure it out yet. Maybe he does deserve a chance with wonderful you, though not every man does and you should get comfortable with the idea.

So let's say he doesn't just show up on your doorstep – you actually found him somewhere. For example, online, through a friend or at work. Don't base what you want on what you find. And don't mold yourself to be what he wants or establish your standards to match the man in front of you. *Who you choose relates to what you've learned about yourself, who you are, and what's important to you.*

Knowing What You Want, Understanding What You Need

Knowing what you want is sometimes the most difficult part of dating. Yes, you can make a big list of characteristics about him, though without some experience, you may not be sure how those things fit with your life and your needs now. And, you may not know what you need so it makes deciding what you want in him even more challenging. It's ok to start from what you know now and let your standards evolve with you.

A Journal Moment

A few questions to help you uncover your own needs.
- In your prior relationships, did you feel supported in a way you responded to?
- Did you feel connected to the relating style (how he communicates, shows concern and interest in you etc.) of men you dated before?
- What's the most important thing about your lifestyle right now? Your flexible schedule, ability to participate with the kids/grandkids, your career direction, where you live, charity work etc?

Writing down these answers may help you get some clarity, so use them when you make your standards list later in the chapter.

Defining Mr. Right *for You*

The clearer you are about what you want, the easier it is to understand who is right for you, recognize him when he appears, and choose to give him a chance. With this approach, the man on your doorstep is there because you deliberately invited him, not because he's the only one who showed up.

There's a big distinction between Mr. Right and Mr. Right *for You*. Lots of women have a Mr. Right in mind and I tend to observe us talking to each other as if it's the same man. Not likely. Most women will say they want a "good man," though who he is, how he lives, and what he's like in a relationship is all different. Yes, there are common themes such as, he knows the difference between right and wrong. However, other things are valued differently such as his profession is important to some women and not to others.

To help you figure out your own standards, follow the *What Do You Know About Him Process* below. The real value of the standards list is the process of taking time to reflect upon what you want to have on it, and more importantly, *why*. It gives you some focus and guidance and makes it easier for you to recognize him when he does cross your path.

Be very careful you're including things on your standards list *you* want in a man and a relationship. Not things other people have on their list, want for you, or gave up on and wish they hadn't settled for. You might be thinking… "Deb, I really don't know what to put on my list. I think I know. But I really don't." That's ok. Part of the dating process includes learning some of these answers. It's a place to start and it'll evolve with you as you become more experienced.

If you've made a list before, use this as an opportunity to dig it out and see if it still fits. These are your standards and will evolve as you do.

What Do You Know About Him

Creating a standards list helps you clear the fog in your head about what's important and what isn't, because it's really easy to confuse the two. The list evolves with the process so go through the sections in the order given. It'll help you think through what you value and narrow down your priorities. We'll start with Mr. Right (otherwise known as Mr. Perfect), recognize the difference in Mr. Right *for You*, and incorporate Mr. He's a Good Man. Your journal is a great place to do this.

Part 1. Mr. Right, aka Mr. Perfect

We'll start with making a comprehensive dreamy list about Mr. Right – otherwise known as Mr. Absolutely Perfect. If you've already done this for yourself, I encourage you to revise it with me as we go through this together. If you've never done this before, think of it like making a shopping list. All the ingredients you need for the perfect man and the relationship you want.

Ok, let'er rip! Given this is Mr. Perfect, write it all down. *Everything* you can possibly think of wanting in your man and your relationship. Don't edit yourself. Dream, dream, dream about Mr. Dream Boat. Or Mr. Rugged. Or Mr. Wealthy. (Yes, I said it 'cause I know some of you are thinking it.) Or Mr. Romantic. Or Mr. Passion. Or Mr. Career. Or Mr. Family. Or whatever your Mr. Perfect is. Hang onto this comprehensive list. We'll use it in all the other sections below.

Here's a few ideas to help you get started on your Mr. Absolutely Perfect list. (In no particular order.)

- Physical appearance (Some of you started here anyway so I put this at the top. The irony is we women get all upset when men start with looks!)

- Age range

- Profession

- Education

- Children

- Parents, Family

- Friends

- Pets

- Character, Values, Priorities, What's important to him.

- Chemistry (The types based on *His Vibe* or *Your Reaction to Him* are later in this chapter.)

- Income, Attitude about Money, Assets

- Communication style. Examples: frequency, length, likes to talk or not, method he uses (phone, text, email, in person), is it a priority for him etc. Don't expect him to communicate like you or like women do, though do expect him to communicate in a way that works for you.

- Relationship style. Examples: attentive, affectionate, leaves you alone to do your thing, likes to spend every night together, wants his own space etc.

- Sex. Examples: attitude, meaning, frequency etc.

- Geographical location

‣ Hobbies, Interests

‣ Things you have in common.

‣ What it means to enjoy his company and be around him

‣ Life history

‣ Religion, Spirituality, Belief System

‣ Lifestyle, Schedule

Part 2. Mr. Right *for You*

Now you have your Mr. Perfect list… let's look at it again. Mr. Perfect doesn't exist for anyone. By the way Mrs. Perfect or Ms. Perfect don't exist either. So, using the 80/20 rule, take a look at your list and figure out the 80% of those things you truly need and want. These are your *Must Haves* and create Mr. Right *for You*. The other 20% becomes the *Nice To Have* column. These are things you're willing to do without though it's possible they could evolve with the relationship depending upon what they are. To really get focused, aim for 70/30 or even 60/40 *Must Have/Nice to Have.*

You're also defining what Mr. He's a Good Man means to you so be sure to include elements of his character. Think of it this way – write down things about him you can see, and include things about him you can't see. The ones you can't see are part of his personality, character, and values. These things need to be experienced to know if he has them, though include them on your list. They are crucial elements of his character that allow him, and you, to grow as people and grow as a couple. An important example is if he's emotionally available - meaning the degree he's willing to be vulnerable and share his feelings versus being guarded and closed off.

Be careful about defining your *Must Haves* all based on activities. Relationships built only on sharing activities (sports, board games, travel, theater, gardening etc.) are not solid relationships. You need to appreciate him for who he is, including his character and values, for a relationship to be real. Yes, have some things in common, though interests can change and if you've based everything on activities, you won't last unless you both adapt together. Of course, he needs to appreciate you for your character and values as well. It's always a two way street.

For the activities on your list, make a note about your expectations. Are they on your list because you want him to share a passion for them, participate occasionally, "let" you go whenever you want, or just know that's part of who you are and how you live your life?

As you develop your list, it's important to acknowledge where you are in life, and how well you know yourself. Relationships include compromise and a desire to work together, not against each other. The key is choosing what you are willing to compromise on and what you're not. This helps you prioritize what to keep on your list as a *Must Have* and what to move to the *Nice To Have* column.

By learning about yourself first, then thinking through your list about who he is, the result should line up with what you need, want and who you choose to become part of your life. As you continue to date, learn more about yourself and what's truly important to you, it's likely your *Must Have* list will become smaller and more focused.

Part 3. Your Deal Breakers

Take your revised list, now the *Must Haves* for Mr. Realistically Right for You, and highlight your *Deal Breakers*. These things are *required* for you to be interested in someone. What your list should contain depends upon you, what you like, how you live, and your general values and belief system. Include things that may seem obvious, like a preference about having or wanting children.

How many *Deal Breakers* you have and what they are depends on you, though including everything on your Mr. Realistically Right for You list doesn't fly. Choose no more than five or so *Deal Breakers*. Dig deep to figure out what is truly so essential you'd *automatically pass* on someone who didn't meet them. Yep – I said *automatically pass*. This list may evolve as you learn more about yourself, though I suspect some of them are part of your personal values.

Careful about too many physical characteristics being *Deal Breakers*. These do evolve with your own maturity and learning what's truly important to you. When I was in my twenties, it would never occur to me to date someone who had a receding hair line or no hair. In my forties, hair or no hair really isn't important in the big picture. I'm far more interested in his character, intelligence, how he lives his life, and how he treats me. If you're thinking hair is a critical *Deal Breaker* for you, put it on your list and understand it narrows your options.

Something to Notice About Your List

The first things you look for in the next relationship are usually what you starved for in the last one. It's typically what's on the top of your *Must Have* list when you're considering who you want in your life. Careful.

Prove It Attitude

While those qualities should probably be on your list, going after them with such spite isn't an attractive emotion, right? Would it be appealing to a man if you are staring him down and wondering if he's ever gonna do what you think he should or what the other guy wouldn't?

Careful of this "prove it" attitude with the next innocent man you meet. That's making him pay for the last one's idiot behavior and wanting vindication from the next one. If you are sticking to your *Deal Breakers*, the one in front of you could have real potential, yet "prove it" energy from you will most likely repel him. Instead, embrace the opportunity to get to know him, without connecting him to the sins of the prior men in your life. Think of the potential adventure before you!

Relationship Goggles

If the first things on your list are all the issues with the last guy, I caution you to reconsider if you're ready to date. (Could be the grumble you made when you wrote them down that tipped me off.) You may think you are ready, though emotionally you aren't quite there and are making a list with your *relationship goggles* on. They are more blinding than beer goggles given relationships goggles include more than physical attributes.

Relationship goggles means you're viewing the next guy based on the last one and measuring the next relationship based on the failures of the last. That's not fair to him, or to you. Until you're ready to move on with a clean slate, perhaps you should do some more work on yourself first.

You see what you look for so if you believe every man is scum, you'll only see the ones who are. And, you'll only choose the ones who are because you can't see any other options. In reality, there are good men. It's a matter of defining what's important to you, taking off the *relationship goggles* of your past, focusing on the good around you, and choosing men who are worthy of a chance with you.

Drama, Negativity, and That Little Voice

Be aware of your *Drama Queen* comfort zones and really be tuned into your body, mind and that little voice in your head trying to tell you something about your choices. Your list should be a positive statement about what you want, not a constant stream about what you don't.

If you are listing more things you don't want than those you do, you haven't quite gotten past judging the last guy, or your last relationship. Take some time to learn the lessons from the experience and translate them into how you'll improve this one. It'll help you shift into a positive state of mind and learn to live in your own power.

Live Your Standards

Having standards and having the *courage to use them* takes different strength. Anyone can write up a list. The question is, did you dig deep into your soul and really reflect upon what's on your list and why? Are the things on your list what you *say* you want or what you *actually* want? Did you consider your *Deal Breakers* and choose things truly important to you?

If so, have the guts to use your standards. When you know what you want, it's much easier to know when you find it… and when you don't. *Sticking by your standards is making a commitment to yourself to honor who you are and what you need.*

How It Might Work

The process might go like this: you meet someone new and learn a little about him. Because you've already identified your *Deal Breakers*, you know some important things you want to learn about him. Most likely, you won't learn all of them when you first meet. It might take some time and several dates depending upon how deep or how personal your *Deal Breakers* are.

Remember, your *Deal Breakers* are those things so important you'll *automatically pass* on dating him if he doesn't match up. If you find yourself questioning your *Deal Breakers*, ask yourself if it's because you're afraid of using them, or if they aren't the right ones.

As you get acquainted, you'll experience how he lives his life, what he values and how he treats you. Along the way, you'll also learn about what's on your *Must Have* list and *Basic Facts* list (more about the *Basic Facts* in the next section). Given you'll have the lists in the back of your mind as a guide, don't take them on your date(s). It's not an inquisition; it's a series of conversations and fun! Be in the moment and enjoy yourself.

With experience comes more knowledge of your priorities and you may discover you want to make some changes to your lists. More things may get moved to the *Nice To Have* list instead of being on the *Must Have* list. Or you may learn what you thought was a *Nice To Have* is really a *Must Have*. Just be careful you don't end up back where we started with the *What Do You Know About Him Process* and a list for Mr. Absolutely Perfect since he doesn't exist.

Focus on the list who is Mr. Right for You – he is imperfect, though right. It'll feel good to know it's your choice and continue to make deliberate decisions that are good for you.

Like Him First

Decide if you like him first, don't wait to decide if you like him based on if he likes you. That's not standing in your own value. That's waiting for him to value you before you use your standards and choose if he gets a chance. If your first criteria is finding out if he likes you, I suspect you're already becoming what he wants instead of being who you are. Knowing if he likes you first may not be on your list, though if it is how you behave, it might as well be.

Your Standards, Not What Others Want

Remember who *you* want, and what he's like should be your list. Not what everyone expects of you, or what everyone else wants for you. Could your friends have some valid ideas? Of course, though be sure you are adding things *you* value. Stand in your own power and choose for yourself.

Online Dating Tip

One tip about online dating - If his headline or profile description says something about a woman he can trust or any other emotional issue… run. He clearly hasn't healed from whatever happened in the last relationship and instead of doing the work to learn and move on, he's wearing his issues like a neon sign. That's *Mr. Project B.A.T.* whining into cyberspace and publishing it for the world to see. The *Drama Queen, Ms. Fix It,* will be drawn to him like a moth to a flame, so be sure you understand your own tendencies and have the courage to steer clear.

This tip applies to women too so don't have an online headline or description like this either. Otherwise, it's *Ms. Project B.A.T.* flashing the neon sign. Instead, take charge of your life, choose to heal from the past, and fully enjoy living in the present. Yes, if men do this they can take down their project sign too.

Picky or Selective

One more note about using your standards – you may be called "picky" when you date using standards, but know there's a big difference between being *picky* and being *selective*. And, there's a big difference in being picky and being selective if you are *"choosing who gets a chance."* Yes, it's subtle and some of you may be thinking it's semantics. However, hear me out.

If you've been called picky in the past, those choices are generally driven by unrealistic expectations and lean toward seeking "perfection." Picky choices are probably rooted in the fear of being hurt again based on hurts from the past. It's the same as when *unrealistic* (perfection) standards become a dating and relationship barrier instead of a guide as discussed in *The Secret - It Starts with You* chapter.

On the other hand, "selective" choices require more thought and means you've taken time to consider what's important to you. Selective is a more proactive decision incorporating your standards and what you value.

A *realistic* standards list helps you be selective, not picky. Selective is choosing Mr. Right for You, while picky is looking for and expecting Mr. Absolutely Perfect. When you make your Mr. Right for You list, *commit to using it*, and adapt it only when you learn something new *you* choose to adjust, don't be swayed by the people who are calling you picky. *Now you know the difference.*

Can't Date a List

No, you can't date a list on a piece of paper, have a relationship with it, nor marry it. And, as I've already said, the purpose of the list is to give you focus and guidance. You won't know his character, observe his values and ethics, learn how he treats you, and feel the chemistry until you meet him, spend time with him, and experience him on dates. Otherwise, you're just creating your own version of *Looks Good on Paper* man.

Well Rounded

When you're on your date, have more to talk about than your work, or your kids, or your house. You don't want to listen to him talk about his career all night, right? You'd like him to have some interests other than his job, or other than sports? Yes, perhaps you love sports too so a sports nut could be a good match, though you get my point. Expecting him to be well rounded, means you need to be as well. You decide what well rounded means. Once again, it starts with you.

Basic Facts

This information speaks to his history, his life now and where he's going. The *Basic Facts* give you an indication of how he lives his life. *I suspect it's the same information he'll want to learn about you for the same reasons.* It might help you fill in your *Mr. Right for You* list and likely includes your *Deal Breakers*.

It's Not an Interrogation

I'm not suggesting you take this *Basic Facts* list and create a checklist for your dates. It's not an interrogation. At its core, a date is a conversation – verbal, body language, behavior and chemistry. There's a lot you can learn about him by listening to him share stories about his life in addition to how he responds to yours. Having these *Basic Facts* in mind means you're paying attention to what you're discovering about him along the way.

The Key

The key to this list is what you do with the information as you learn it. If any of these *Basic Facts* are part of your *Deal Breakers*, and he doesn't meet them, you're done. Be an adult and politely say this isn't a match for you and move on. You'd want him to have enough respect for you to say something, right? Don't belabor the point though he may want to know why, just like you would. If you have a friendship started with this man, perhaps a conversation could help both of you learn. If you don't, use our own judgment if you think it's a good idea to continue talking. Otherwise, respectfully end it and move on.

Basic Facts List

- Name with correct spelling, including middle name at some point.
- That he's single and available.
- That he's straight.
- Type of relationship he's seeking (no strings fun, casual dating, something with potential, something serious).

- Physical characteristics (height, body type, hair color or none, eye color).

- Phone number, email address.

- Age.

- Where he lives (general area, don't need an address if you've just met, eventually yes).

- Where he grew up.

- Family, parents, siblings and what birth order he is.

- Education.

- Profession, job, career, business; does he travel for work.

- What he does for fun.

- Does he have pets, what are they and how does he feel about them (for example, member of the family or animal?)

- Does he own his home?

- Does he live alone or with a roommate or with family?

- Does he have any dreams or things he wants to do in his life?

- Does he have children? How many, ages, gender, and where to do they live.

- How long has he been at his current job and if he likes it.

- If previously married, how long was he married and how long has he been divorced and what is his attitude about it.

- If recently out of a relationship, how long were they together and how long has it been since they broke up and his attitude about it.

‣ His spiritual or religious beliefs and how he practices them.

‣ Eventually, if you are getting serious, you both need to discuss your financial situation - attitudes about saving versus spending, having a budget or not, investments, and general philosophy about money.

The context of the *Basic Facts* varies based on you. For example, if you're a "live in the moment" person, the item about him having dreams and looking ahead takes on a different meaning. So for you, this *Basic Fact* may change to "his attitude about living now or looking ahead." You decide if you prefer his attitude match yours, be different than yours, or if it matters.

Another example is if he has children. Say he has two kids. And, since you know this information, one of the things you can observe is how important are they to him. If in your conversations with him he never mentions them, what's that about? If I was dating someone with kids, I would want to know if he is a good father to them. It speaks volumes about his values.

Chemistry

Chemistry is definitely a heart emotion – not much common sense or logic. Some of you may be thinking it's a body or soul feeling, and I agree. Your physical response to his aura or energy or "air" is also a heart thing. There are different opinions about how chemistry is felt when you're dating, and when you're in a relationship.

I've heard everything from "If there's no chemistry right from the beginning, I'm not interested" to "There must be some chemistry, though it can also build over time as you get to know someone." Yes, you want a spark between you though the bigger and hotter, the more likely it's just lust and probably means you'll ignore all the things that don't work about you two together. Eventually, it'll burn itself out.

Don't make *relationship* decisions based solely on lust. A *date*, perhaps. Mr. Right Now, most likely. Though if you're seeking a long-term relationship, making choices based on lust, or how long it's been since you had sex, or the quivering feeling in your knees isn't going to take you in the direction you say you want. It could create lots of short-term fun! Just remember, if you start something casual that includes sex, it may not become anything else.

Make good choices for yourself. Not what others believe or according to their standards. Make them based on what you value and what you truly want from the man you are considering. On the other hand, if the spark is such a dud you can't even light the match, that's not going to work either.

Here's some food for thought about chemistry types from two perspectives: *Your Reaction to Him* and *His Vibe*. It's not likely every man you meet will fit into one of the types, though these general descriptions may help you understand who you're attracted to.

Chemistry Based on Your Reaction to Him

Rip Each Other's Clothes Off – He's smokin' hot and smoldering… this is lust.

Friend – Have fun together, share ideas, have things in common, and enjoy each other's company. You feel good around him except there's no spark.

Intrigue – This feeling of intrigue might be a disguise for something interesting only to learn it's the bad boy *B.A.T.* attraction.

Spark of Desire – There's a heat between you, plus you notice there's potential for who you are looking for using your Mr. Right for You standards. Conversation feels like a connection and the notion you may understand each other.

None – This spells move on. Enough said.

Chemistry Based on His Vibe

Manly Man, Man's Man – These men are very masculine, strong and protective. They can and do care, though probably aren't into talking about feelings. "Strong, silent type" could be the stereotype.

Sensitive Man – These men not only ask about your feelings, the perceptive ones already know what you're thinking. They can be strong and protective, it's just not as obvious like the *Manly Man* vibe.

Blend – A *Sensitive, Manly Man.* Most likely they show their sensitive side only to you, and only in private. In public they behave more like a manly man. Their interests may or may not suggest they are *Manly Men* or *Sensitive Men.* That part is a toss up. Generally, in my experience, it's their attitude that gives away their nature.

Rough Around the Edges – This man is a *guy* who lives like a true bachelor, doesn't think to ask or plan ahead, though probably has good intentions. Could be a little immature in how he runs his life, more commonly referred to as "he'll need lots of training."

Refined – Better social skills than *Rough Around the Edges* and probably has sophisticated interests. Easier to take him places without fear of what might happen to embarrass you. Could be a combo of any of the rest though probably skews toward Sensitive.

One more thing to consider about chemistry: You can have an attraction to the bad boy *B.A.T.* chemistry, though with a *good man* who has potential for Mr. Right for You, you have a *connection and an attraction*. Might make a note on your Mr. Right for You list about chemistry.

Signs He Could Be a Good Choice

▸ Responsive and respectful of you.

▸ Values the real you (of course you need to show him the real you for this to matter).

▸ Initiates contact, follows up.

▸ Does what he says he will.

▸ Emotionally healthy, not perfect or without any issues, though has coped with his past, decisions he's made and continues to recognize life goes on.

▸ Genuinely apologizes when he screws up – not just because he's trying to get out of the dog house with you, he actually means it.

▸ Brings out the best in you, and you in him.

▸ Encourages you to become the best you can be.

▸ The answer to the question, "what has he done to deserve me" is easy and abundant with great things.

▸ Consistently good to you. (Personally, I like it better than infrequent grand gestures.)

▸ He could be anywhere and he chooses to be with you because of his genuine interest in you.

▸ You feel comfortable with him and aren't constantly worried about what your hair looks like. (Unless that's just how you are.)

▸ Easy conversation. (Be careful not to go too far with judging this. I don't mean nervous silences, or shaking knees cause it's your first date with him.)

▸ Who you are when you are around him - are you yourself or are you behaving like someone you think he wants? If you find yourself becoming someone else because of demands he's making or expectations he has that don't match your authentic self – this is a reverse sign and it means run. You want to truly feel like yourself when you're together, and when you're not.

▸ You have fun together.

▸ He can see past the boobs – If he can see beyond the boobs, he's actually looking for someone beyond a physical attraction. Yes, he still wants a physical attraction, plus he wants to learn about you as a person. If you are seeking a relationship, watch for the man who can see past the boobs. Those who can't need to work on their social skills or are probably looking for something very casual. You decide if his attitude matches what you want and have the courage to dump him if it doesn't.

Alerts He's Not a Good Choice

▸ How you feel when you are around him – uneasy, questioning, wondering?

▸ Your body reaction, energy level, breathing, tension.

‣ Always justifying, nervous, trying to be something you aren't. This could also be your insecurity shining its bright light so take the time to figure out the difference.

‣ Feeling like you have to ask if he wants to be in the relationship. It should be abundantly clear. In *his own way* you should be learning about and appreciating (it's another alert if you aren't and don't), he's communicating his interest and desire to be on a date or in this relationship with you. This doesn't mean he gets it exactly right and communicates the way you want him to – it means he's doing it his own way and you're getting the message. Of course, if you feel like you always have to ask, it could be your insecurity showing so be aware if it's your issue or his.

‣ When he shares something about himself or his life and you have this little voice inside your head saying you don't believe him and feel like something is fishy.

‣ You're observing *B.A.T. Signs* or *B.A.T. Types*.

Coping with the B.A.T.s

Being aware of *B.A.T. Signs* and *B.A.T. Types* means you're sifting through some themes in attitudes and behavior. Unfortunately, this process can be difficult since there's no exact formula. Combine this with the reasoning that every person is unique and it creates the easy *"He's Different"* excuse from Chapter 2. Be smart and choose better.

Self awareness is crucial. The more you know yourself, what you want and listen to your gut, the easier it will be to spot *B.A.T. Signs* and *B.A.T. Types*. Listening to what he says and what he doesn't, may help. After you spot one, be deliberate about evaluating his *B.A.T.* risk and what to do *this* time. Care enough about yourself to stop choosing B.A.T.s.

Know what you want, both in a relationship and about the character of the man you are seeking. This defines the standards you're evaluating the possibilities against.

I Don't Want To Scare Him Off

"Don't want to scare him off" is a phrase I've heard, and have used myself in the past. Here's the thing - if a man wants to be in a relationship with you he won't be scared off. Now, I'm not saying propose to him or declare you want to marry him on the first date. Or call him constantly and show up where he works. Or drive by his house. Or call his friends. Or have lunch with his Mother he hasn't introduced you to yet. (Yes, I've heard them all.) That would scare anyone off. Be reasonable.

There is some art and science to the dating process, though if you want a relationship and he doesn't, believe him and choose someone who is looking for a relationship. If he "scares" easily, it may be his issue not yours. Or, it's an excuse and he's really *Mr. Vanishing Man B.A.T. Type*. Or, perhaps you just aren't the right woman for him. Regardless, you're one step closer to the one who is.

He's Great! Well... Except for....

Choosing to date someone you want to change is a waste of time. Even if you're trying to expand his fashion sense, you're trying to change him. No one, including you, wants to date someone who wants to change them - like they aren't good enough to be accepted the way they are. Why would you choose someone you want to change anyway? Because he's right in front of you and you think he's your only shot? If that's the case, it's your insecurity showing.

If you like everything except... better get very clear about the X factor you don't like 'cause you may not find it in him. If the X factor is a *Deal Breaker*, you're done anyway so why are you trying to change it in him? If the X factor is a *Nice To Have* stop obsessing over something that's not crucial to you. If the X factor is on your *Must Have* list, get very clear about how important it really is to you.

If you decide the missing X factor is a priority for you - here's the faith and courage coming into the picture. Take a bold step, make a good choice and move on to someone you don't feel like you have to change so he meets your expectations. *There are a lot of men in the world and you're only looking for one.*

Love is Blind Only if You Are

Love is blind when people throw up their hands and decide they have no choices. They don't have any standards, or don't use the ones they have. Often, lust is mistaken for love and it determines who they let in their life. I'm not saying don't have the torrid affair with the smokin' hot man. Just realize you are having a torrid affair with the smokin' hot man and know it's probably not going anywhere but to the bedroom.

Courage

As I said, having standards and actually having the courage to use them are different things. I've spoken with several women who say they have standards, and then choose to date men who don't meet them. My guess is your *Cinderella Head* is talking or perhaps your inner *Drama Queen* is showing. You certainly aren't valuing yourself enough to choose a man worthy of you and are *settling* for what you can get. *Give yourself permission to use your standards.*

Weeding Them Out

Choosing who gets a chance starts with weeding out those who don't fit your *Deal Breakers*. Choosing who gets a chance is also about learning to recognize who might have potential based on your *Must Have* list. Defend your heart and yourself using your *Deal Breakers* and the B.A.T. *Signs* and B.A.T. *Types*.

The Shift

Let's say he meets your *Deal Breakers*, you've assessed the B.A.T. risk and decide you're ok with it, and you have some chemistry with him -- now start to look for things that *are* what you want, versus continuing to focus on what you don't.

It's a subtle shift, though crucial for the relationship to continue. This is the point where love sprouts and you are no longer blind because you've been paying attention to your *Deal Breakers* and those things on your *Mr. Right for You* list. Enjoy getting to know each other and have some fun!

You might be wondering when does this shift happen? How will I know it's time? There's no exact timeline. If you like him, he meets your *Deal Breakers*, has the character you respect, and treats you the way you cherish in a relationship, the shift can happen at any time. Remember, you create the shift within yourself. This isn't something you discuss with him. It's about you acknowledging your own focus points and making a deliberate choice to focus in the present, with the possibility of the future.

Open the Door

Now don't logic yourself to death and become so closed off you forget the possibilities of butterflies in your stomach or the silly school girl grin on your face when you think of him. This is especially risky if you've been through a breakup when you're more likely to lock the door on emotions for fear of getting hurt again. Or, you open the door so wide you're walking around with every hurt that's ever happened to you on a t-shirt. The answer lies in the middle where the door is open and inviting yet not so much you're an emotional wreck, or so closed you are too guarded. What the "middle" means depends upon you. *Love is Blind Only if You Are* includes being blind to yourself.

Expectations

Choosing who gets a chance is also about understanding your own expectations. Are you being realistic about what you expect of him or are you actually expecting Prince Charming? Or, are your standards and expectations still low because you don't believe in you yet or believe that you deserve the best. Eeek! That's on the road to *settling*.

A Journal Moment

▸   How does it feel to have a *What Do You Know About Him* standards list?

‣ Will you give yourself permission to use them? Why or why not? What will you change?

‣ Have you had *Love is Blind Only if You Are* relationships where you only saw what you wanted or wished for instead of what actually was? What will you do differently this time?

The Answer is Obvious

Sometimes the answer of who we choose or who we don't is more obvious than we let it be. We justify the crappy behavior and lame excuses under the guise of forgiveness. We all make mistakes, forgiveness is important, and we certainly shouldn't expect perfection from men or ourselves. However, justifying his idiotic behavior because addressing it means scary changes for you doesn't help your life.

If you are dissecting the great things and looking for anything amiss, it's likely you're convinced the good won't last. You probably believe it's just a matter of time before everything blows up. Seems the root of this problem is fear.

If something is really amiss, have the courage to make the hard choice to change things. Whatever that may mean. If things are good, enjoy it and stop worrying!

Men should want to earn a relationship and spend time with you. Not as a test, or some "I'm better than you" game. It means you value yourself enough to expect him to treat you well and if he wasn't, isn't or doesn't, you choose someone else.

What Will You Choose?

Default	Deliberate
‣ Take what you can get.	‣ Have the courage to use your standards.
‣ Lust defines your choices.	
‣ No one else you know uses any standards, or sticks to the ones they say the have. They just date whoever they meet - even if he isn't really who they want. So, you just follow suit because it's easier and doesn't rock the boat with your friends.	‣ Define your *Deal Breakers*, *Must Haves* and *Nice To Haves* for *Mr. Right for You*.
	‣ Pay attention to his *Basic Facts*.
	‣ To live your standards, you won't really know if he's a fit for you until you date him, feel the chemistry, experience how he lives his life, and how he treats you.

This Time

Use these affirming statements as encouragement when you need it or to celebrate deliberate changes you're making *this time*.

‣ *I am strong and believe in myself enough to use my standards and choose a man worthy of a chance with me.*

‣ *I believe in my Deal Breakers and will automatically pass on men who don't meet them.*

‣ *My Must Have and Nice to Have lists are as complete as I know today and I commit to using them.*

‣ *I will update my standards as I learn more about myself and what's truly important to me.*

CHAPTER 8

Danger! Danger! You're About to Settle.

Settling is when you ignore your standards and let Mr. Right In Front of You become part of your life. This *I'm-about-to-settle-danger-zone* is anchored by dating burnout and sheer frustration with the whole dating process… the time it takes… the blind dates you agreed to… the outfits you planned. It's especially irritating since you took the time to learn about yourself, understand the *B.A.T. Signs* and *B.A.T. Types*, defined your standards for *Mr. Right for You* and they are reasonable things… and it all comes down to not meeting the right man. Now you're convinced he doesn't exist or he lives on another planet.

The *I'm-about-to-settle-danger-zone* might be aggravating enough to lower your standards so far you pick a man "who'll do." On top of that, you throw up your hands (sometimes literally) since you can't control anything anyway, yet you are still seeking someone special in your life. This is usually followed by slumping over on the couch with a groan. And, maybe some ice cream. Or chocolate. Or a cocktail. Or a combination.

This is the time you need your *real friends*… and I don't mean you need them to hook you up. I mean you need them to know you well enough to leave you alone if you need it, to take you out for dinner when you need it, and to make you laugh when you need it. Most importantly, you need them to encourage you to keep trying if you want a relationship, and let you know there's nothing wrong with choosing to take a break or choosing to be single. *Notice I said choosing, not giving up.*

The Mr. Good Enough Trap

Undoubtedly, there are very lonely moments in dating – especially for those of you who are seeking an actual relationship. Ya, this is where it would be so much easier to *settle*, to identify Mr. Good Enough and let him stay in your life. You know who he is - the one you like, but there's just something not quite right. The one who almost meets your *Deal Breakers*, except that one…. It would be so nice to have him around when you've had an awful day and need someone to talk to who genuinely believes in you, holds you, and understands you even when you're sobbing out of sheer frustration with your life. It's so tempting to see Mr. Good Enough through the lens of what you wish he was instead of who he really is.

What Fuels the Trap

The "I'm about to settle" trap is fueled by lonesomeness, being tired of cooking for one, wanting someone to go to the movies with without having to worry if it's a date or not, and the desire to have someone in your corner. And, it could be a deeper issue like feeling unloved or there's no one to believe in you. It's also fueled by changes in your career, or the feeling that it's going nowhere. If you're a Mom on top of all that, you might throw in a healthy dose of Mom-guilt for not being married to their father and stir. The concoction you just created is single, lonely and desperate.

I don't remember anyone ever saying "desperate" was a positive, productive emotion leading to quality choices or attracting quality men. Your emotional state is the primary reason you're pondering settling.

It Will Pass

The best news is *this trap will pass.* Believe in yourself, even when you're bawling on the couch about how much you hate your life right now and you'd like things to be different. Give yourself permission to have a *"This really sucks!"* moment, then pick yourself up and live your life. You are still a vital, intelligent, accomplished woman of substance and when you wake up from the *settling danger zone* you're currently in, you'll see, and believe, that again. Ask your *real friends* for help. It's what they are there for.

Fighting That "He'll Do" Feeling

This is a toughie. It's the feeling that while you don't want just anyone, you are also tired of being single. You have great friends, yet when you're at home... by yourself... and it's quiet... and you don't want to clean your house as a distraction... and you'd rather have someone in your life to spend time with... to think about... to have fun with.... *Sigh.* So... the next phrase that pops into your head when you're thinking about the man you're dating is "He'll do..." followed by a *heavier sigh.* This ambivalent, "I guess it'll be okay," reaction is a clue you're about to settle.

I'm not talking about the moment when you actually find Mr. Right for You, are scared to death of this new path you are on and trying to convince yourself "it'll be ok" as a soothing method for your fear. Part of that feeling is excitement and genuinely looking forward to your life with him. When you settle, none of that exists. Mr. I Settled will simply fill a void, even though he's not the man you seek. Doesn't make him a bad guy, just means he isn't Mr. Right for You.

But, What If...

I suspect some of you got to this exact place in a relationship and *caved*. You stepped outside of your own strength, stopped believing in what you deserve, and *settled for the man in front of you*. You may find yourself in the same risky, emotionally weak state of mind and heart again in your life - still single or single again and wondering "what if...."

If you've been dating, you catch yourself reviewing all the men you cast aside or the ones who seemed interested in you, but you can't remember why you weren't interested in them. So, you start running through the list. Why didn't I like him? What was wrong with that one? Why wasn't I attracted to the other one? Why didn't I respond to his online profile?

Coulda, Woulda, Shoulda

It all seems to blur and you find yourself recounting all the men you could've or should've given the time of day to instead of dismissing them for what seem to be insignificant reasons. You probably hadn't done any work on your *Mr. Right for You* list at that point of your life so you didn't know the difference between your *Must Haves* or *Nice to Haves*, and hadn't defined your *Deal Breakers*. Now, you're considering a man who *should* be dismissed yet you're about to cave and allow him to stay in your life.

Yes, maybe you have made some mistakes, assumptions or otherwise unobservant decisions regarding men who were around you in your past. However, now is not the time to lower your standards and settle for someone "who'll do." If you've settled before, you are in grave danger of doing it again. If you haven't settled yet, you're in grave danger of starting a *really bad pattern.*

BE CAREFUL when you get into these moods. Call your friends, your mother, your brother even, but do not call anyone you've dated before thinking another go-round with him is better than being by yourself. If another round with Mr. I've Dated Him Before was a good idea, you would've thought about it when you were happy, not when you're feeling low and alone. If you ever decide to date someone you've dated before, do it because you are different, you have grown and he has too… enough it might work this time. Don't do it because it's a last resort shot of desperation.

It's the Lonely Talking

The fuel of this fire is still being lonely. It's normal and not unusual. And, it can change. However, if you listen to the lonely talking, you may confuse feeling comforted by someone with actually liking him. It can create false devotion and misguided emotional connections like mistaking lonely for attraction. You may not even like the man in front of you, but your emotions and judgment are clouded by your desire to have someone in your life to take away the lonesome feeling.

Choosing someone who isn't good for you, but is already in your life is very easy and convenient. It is so much simpler than using your standards and mustering the strength to find a man who meets them. Staying with Mr. I Settled means you aren't focused on what you want, just on what you found right now or until someone else comes along.

The problem is it keeps you from being open to the one you really want, given your effort and some degree of emotion is tied to Mr. I Settled. It's a vicious cycle and hard to break until you've stopped long enough to examine your choices and how they create your life. *Otherwise you'll continue to settle for what you find instead of choosing what you want.*

Does He Like Me?

Seems the most hated part of dating is when you are interested in someone and you don't know if they return the sentiment. It's the part where you feel jittery and smile a lot because you've let yourself get a little bit excited about someone new... but... hold on. Then, the feeling of "I'm-afraid-to-go-there-because-I-don't-know-if-he-likes-me-back" takes over. You fret and stew trying to figure out if it's "nothing serious," are you "just friends," or if you "have potential." Your next thought might be *is it really worth it?*

If you stop there, settling can mean you gave up because you were too chicken to find out if it could be something. That's fear talking because if you get what you want, you have something to lose.

Yes or No Box

It's kinda like elementary school when you passed a note to the boy you liked and asked him to mark the "yes" or "no" box behind the question, "Do you like me?" Sometimes I think there is some merit to that method, though obviously I don't suggest you use it. It saves face to face rejection in case the answer is no, and it builds some excitement for both people if the answer is yes.

As adults, what you don't know is if the answer is yes, does it mean "yes" on an ongoing basis or just right now? As in "This is fun for me, but not something I plan to continue," but I'm-not-going-to-tell-you-that-because-then-you-won't-be-fun-anymore. Or, is it "Yes, I'm interested and I want to continue getting to know you" – which you may translate into "I feel the same way you do... intrigued, interested and enjoy spending time together." So you wonder, which answer is it?

It's Kinda Scary

This seems to be the part of dating that's worse than choosing someone because having feelings for him puts you out on a limb and feels *vulnerable*. You've chosen him, he meets your *Deal Breakers*, and you like him, though you aren't sure if you are just friends and aren't going to be anything else, or if you both think there's potential for more. Of course, that's assuming that you both are looking for something more or are open to something more.

Careful here – everything is connected. This uncertain feeling and fear of potential rejection is connected to "it's too hard" or "now it's kinda scary" and I-don't-want-to-have-to-figure-it-out. That means: you (or he) will just stop, find someone else or give up. None of those options honor the emotions you have for this man who gave you butterflies in your stomach. Sad.

The Remedy

You have to trust someone at some point. You can't doubt every man you date who meets your *Deal Breakers*, has low B.A.T. risk, have some chemistry with, and are learning about the *Must Haves* on your list. The remedy is patience and choosing someone you could, at some point, have a conversation with about your feelings, his feelings and what you are both looking for. Then you'll have the answer about his interest in you and yours in him. Are you sure you want it? See – it can be a big emotional circle if you let it.

A crucial part about learning to trust him is being able to *trust yourself* and your decisions. Does this guarantee it will work out? Nope. Trusting yourself does mean you are genuinely standing in your own power and have made a deliberate decision to give it a chance.

When Things Get Murky

Here's a Scenario

He wants to be around her for his own selfish entertainment. Not get married. Not have more kids, given he already has two. She wants to get married and maybe have kids.

He doesn't want to commit though he behaves as if he's in an exclusive relationship. She wants to commit and only have him in her life.

She's putting up with his uncertainty, distance and lack of emotional attachment because??? Most likely she's dreaming he'll change, evolve and suddenly declare he wants her exclusively. It's her choice and her risk to take. Are you wondering why she would put up with being treated this way? She's showing her *Drama Queen* tendencies.

He's putting up with her insecurity, stirring things up and generally negative attitude about life. He leads her to believe he's there for her, and she believes him. In reality, he's getting laid, he knows he doesn't have any emotional attachment to her and he likes it that way. You might have noticed he's showing *B.A.T. Signs* and may be one of the *B.A.T. Types*.

If you are on one side of this or the other – you decide what's best for you. Lop sided emotional investments either evolve or die, from one side or the other. If you are the one who is emotionally attached and want to keep dating someone who isn't, you can decide to take the risk and let it evolve. Or end it, and stop investing time and emotion. Especially if he's showing signs he doesn't care about you.

If you are the one who is enjoying the time, though don't have any deep feelings, only you can decide to string him along or be honest with him. You don't want men to use you, so think very carefully about using them. Your *real friends* could help you see things from both sides perhaps.

Regardless of which side of this scenario you're on, the best thing you can do is recognize its happening. This allows you to make deliberate decisions that are good for you and not settle for what you have or what is convenient instead of what you want.

What Was I Thinking???

Here's Another Scenario

This time you stuck to your *Deal Breakers* and gave him a shot.

Except for the one Deal Breaker you decided to make an exception about... and didn't tell your friends about... because you knew they would call you out... and you really like him... and everyone deserves a chance... and what if he'll change for me?.... Wow. Big time justifying with your *Cinderella Head*, ignoring your standards, not standing in your own power, nor believing in your own value.

If you're about to settle for someone who doesn't give you what you need, have the character you respect, or lives a lifestyle you want to be part of — *what the hell are you doing?* You might even say you love him and ignore the fact that the life you would have together is not what you say you want. How does staying with him honor you, what you want and what you deserve? This goes back to staying true to yourself, listening to your *real friends* when they are trying to help you see things more clearly, and making the tough decision to walk away from a man who isn't good for you - *even if you have feelings for him.*

When you reach the point of screaming to yourself "WHAT WAS I THINKING?!?!?" – Congratulations!!! It means you have recognized your own standards and have decided to actually use them. Questioning yourself so you can learn from your choices is productive. Questioning yourself and reliving every moment and every conversation and continuing to beat yourself up over the choices you made, is not.

You'll know you are learning and growing in the dating process when you are able to recognize the issues creating this *"what was I thinking"* feeling sooner rather than later. You know - take action when you know something doesn't add up instead of waiting until the end when you feel duped or foolish because you saw the signs and let them slide. Most likely, you buried your head in the sand, ignored the obvious, and just hoped everything would change.

You'll know better this time.

When Good Isn't Right

This is a difficult situation for your head and your heart, though it is an example of knowing yourself, trusting your instincts and your decisions, and having the courage to use your standards. You might discover a man who is good, kind, and decent... and he still isn't the right one.

This happened to me. I met someone who was consistently good to me. He called when he said he would, showed up when he said he would, brought me food when I was sick, and even offered great ideas when I was stressed about work.

You may be thinking – "He sounds pretty great. Why wasn't he right?" As I experienced how he lived his life and his belief system, it didn't spell a shot at "forever." My instincts told me he wasn't the one for me, and I learned he didn't meet one of my *Deal Breakers*.

On top of that, we were both on the brink of making another common mistake: thinking we could change things about the other person. It wasn't a direct conversation, though I knew it was in the back of both of our minds. Is it possible someone will change the way you want them to? Sure it is. Likely? Probably not. Is it fair to expect them to? No. He deserved to be loved and accepted for the person he is and so do I.

It was difficult for me to end a relationship with a *good man*, but I knew in my very conflicted heart he wasn't the *right man* for me. Do not settle for good, when you know it isn't right. It would've been a mistake for both of us.

Settling for Mr. Good Enough is not choosing Mr. Right for You.

Dating B.A.T.s

If you choose to date *B.A.T.s*, go into it with your eyes wide open. You may be a temporary crutch for him, or the stereotypical "rebound" woman. Just be aware of your decisions and don't wrap your whole life around him. Actually, don't do that for a *non-B.A.T.* either. Meaning, live your life and be aware of your emotions, how you truly feel about him and what makes you feel that way. Be aware if he's ready for the same things you are.

One of the snafus in dating, especially with some *B.A.T.s*, is they don't know they are *B.A.T.s*. Mr. *Just Divorced B.A.T.*, for example, will tell you he's over his ex-wife and ready to move on. And, in his mind, he probably believes that. The issue is he doesn't know what he doesn't know. And, you don't know either. That's the risk to evaluate. As you gain more experience and learn from the choices you've made, you'll be able to decide whether a particular *Just Divorced B.A.T.* is a road you want to go down. Or, you can choose a different path.

There are other *B.A.T.s* who are malicious jerks who know they are malicious jerks and choose to be exactly that. There is nothing about dating this type of *B.A.T.* that honors you. Nothing. Have more self respect and don't settle.

I've Invested So Much Time Already

On how many occasions have you heard women, and men for that matter, say, "Well, we've been together so long... we decided to get married." Using how long you've been together as a reason for nuptials is serious settling. It's like you didn't even make the decision, you're letting the time invested in the relationship make it for you.

Basically, this decision says, "I'm going to spend the rest of my life with someone I may not actually want to marry, yet I'm going to anyway because we've spent X years together." So you're trading the rest of your life because you don't want to give up what you believe you've already "invested?" Seems like a disproportionate investment to me. Yes, it'll hurt to end a relationship that's lasted a long time. Though I'm certain it's better than choosing to marry the man and commit to spending ALL of your years with him.

I've heard it many times... "Well, we didn't know what else to do so we got married. Seemed like the next step." Instead of, "I'm excited to spend the rest of my life with him." If you've done this already in your life, you've experienced what I'm talking about here. If you haven't, please don't. Stop. Think. And carefully consider what you truly want and if it's really with this man you've spent X years with just because you've spent X years with him.

Ultimate Settling

Ultimate settling is when you choose a man you don't like, don't respect, don't love or don't enjoy being around - or whatever version you've created that makes it settling for you -PLUS you've become something you're not in the process. So not only have you chosen a man you don't want to be with, you've lost yourself too, and the only thing left is a wish things would be different. That's an extremely high price to pay for a version of "love" that's the furthest from it. It's a high price just to be able to say you are in a relationship, or worse yet, you are married.

Fear of being alone is the reason you scraped the bottom of the barrel and accepted the lowest common denominator of possibilities for yourself instead of having enough strength to believe you deserve and can have something more from a man, and for yourself. It's the same as if you are waiting for the most screwed up *MEGA B.A.T.* possible to suddenly become a "family man" who is monogamous, loving and faithful to you. That if you can get *him* to love and commit to you, it's even more meaningful and you are even more validated by his choice to be with you. (Your *Drama Queen* is showing.)

Stop. It's time to *wake up*. You can validate yourself. You don't have to be in a relationship to have love in your life or feel needed. Sex maybe, depending upon your beliefs on that topic. Relationship, no. There is love all around you with your friends, family, or neighbors if you open your eyes and look. You still have people in your life who believe in you, care for you and want you to have the best life possible.

149

Danger Signs

It's when you are tired and on the brink of selling out that you may cave on your standards and decide they aren't that important after all. Be careful of issues you are ignoring. They create regret later on.

Also be careful of other people influencing you to settle. It's especially easy to be vulnerable to other people's opinions about your standards when you are tired and worn out from the process. After all, some people think if you won't settle, you won't compromise. And, they'll go on to say if you won't compromise you won't ever have a successful relationship. I can't say STOP listening to them fast enough.

Here's why: being unwilling to settle means you have standards that honor yourself and what you need. Relationships are full of compromise though as I said before, the key is what you choose to compromise about. If you are about to settle, we're not talking about compromising on where you are going to dinner tonight. We're talking about big stuff that means you are compromising yourself, what you need, and what's important to you. It means you've chosen a man who doesn't meet your standards and creates a life you don't even want.

You Are About to Settle If...

‣ You find yourself thinking, "Is this it? Is this the relationship I said I wanted all this time and this is all it is?" Or, "Is this all there is?"

‣ You may also be thinking "I can't be myself around him." or "I can't become who I want to be if I'm with him."

‣ You agree with your friends who tell you he's "good enough." Yikes.

‣ You don't trust him.

‣ You don't respect him.

‣ He doesn't have ethics or values you embrace.

‣ He's not reliable; you wonder if he will he stick around during the hard parts of life.

‣ You're not sure he's able to manage his life or cope with life events.

‣ He's stuck in the past and doesn't treat you like he's ready to move on.

‣ Still defines himself by his friends, parents and their opinions – not thinking for himself.

‣ You justify staying together based on how long you've dated, not how you feel about him and if he meets your standards.

‣ You let your biological clock pick the man in front of you because he's there and you're not getting any younger.

‣ You toss aside your standards list and your *Cinderella Head* takes over.

‣ You don't believe him when he shares information about himself, answers questions about his life or how he lives it. That little voice inside your head telling you something is wrong is going to get very tired if you settle for this man and let him in your life.

See the *B.A.T. Signs* chapter for more ways you may be settling.

Face the Truth

If any of these ring a bell, it's time to *face the truth*. You are a wonderful woman with courage to make good, deliberate decisions for yourself. If he isn't the one, give yourself permission to end it and walk away.

After you face the truth and end things, take time to heal. Just remember the more time you spend moping around and wondering what could've been, the less energy you spend enjoying today and looking forward to what could be.

A Journal Moment

‣ Consider your dates and/or relationships – what danger signs sound familiar? Did you have the courage to end it? What happened? What would you do differently this time?

‣ These danger signs may apply to life events outside of your love life so consider other decisions in your life and if you see danger signs. Did you ignore them or embrace them and make a deliberate choice? How will you use those lessons this time?

Where IS he??? The good man who's great in bed?

Hang in there. Hang in there. Hang in there.

It's an annoying piece of advice to receive… believe me I know. It's true though. Continue to work on you, stick to your standards, enjoy your life and be open to the possibilities.

What Will You Choose?

Default	Deliberate
‣ Ignore the settling danger signs.	‣ Remember you have standards to honor yourself and what you need.
‣ Let lonely choose who you date.	
‣ Invite Mr. Good Enough or Mr. He'll Do into your life.	‣ Face the truth of the settling danger signs.
‣ Ignore your Mr. Right for You standards because of dating burnout.	‣ Use your strength and walk away.
	‣ Keep trying.

This Time

Use these affirming statements as encouragement when you need it or to celebrate deliberate changes you're making *this time*.

‣ *I recognize the danger signs of settling and have the courage to choose differently.*

‣ *I decide who gets a chance, and I won't let others influence me to settle.*

‣ *If I am on a date or in a relationship and feel the danger signs, I have the strength to examine my options and make a deliberate decision that honors me.*

CHAPTER 9

Breaking Up

Unfortunately, dating wouldn't exist without breaking up. Everyone would just marry the first person they met in their life and that would be that.

Thankfully, dating does exist and we do have choices. So, like most things in life, you take the good with the bad and obviously breaking up is a bad part. The rejection alone spins your heart and your head in multiple directions. You're wondering how it could've happened, why it happened, and what you coulda/shoulda/woulda done to prevent it. Or, you're wondering why you didn't do it sooner.

If it's a divorce or the breakup of a long-term relationship – every area of your life is impacted - your job, business, family, kids, home, friends, finances, and self-worth are all affected in great ways and horrible ways and all simultaneously. In this hurt, confused, angry, and frustrated emotional state, you may spend a lot of time looking for validation from anywhere you can get it. Mostly you're trying to make sense out of the situation and figure out what happened.

Repeated heartbreak, being dumped or even dumping someone you cared for all add up to shuddering at the thought of trying again. This is the fear of being hurt, memory of the pain, and wondering if it's really worth it. Or, worrying you'll make another mistake and end up dumped again. Could also be a little dash of wondering if you're really worth it and questioning your own value.

Your decisions are generally emotional after a breakup and not likely ones you would make for yourself if you had your head on straight. Be careful about making big life changing decisions before you've had some time to cope.

Have an Anthem

An important healing tip - have an anthem for yourself. Play it every time you need a pick me up, are leading an important meeting, going to a parent-teacher conference, the grocery store, or playing with the grandkids. Whenever you need to be you, without the emotional toll of the breakup.

Eventually, you'll reach the point where you are standing in your own power again and create some peace for yourself. Healing is a process and how long it takes depends on you.

It's Just Over

It doesn't matter which side of the breakup you are on, you still broke up. Yes, it's easier if it was your idea, though if you thought he was someone you could be in a long-term relationship with and you were wrong – it still smarts.

If you were the one who was dumped – it hurts even more. The vulnerable risk you took to have the relationship combined with the feelings you have for him cuts like betrayal.

Ever heard this – or maybe said this - "What does he see in *her*???" You might already know the answer to the question - you just don't like it because he didn't choose you. If he doesn't believe you are for him, then he isn't for you either. Being bitter about a breakup only makes you look foolish because he doesn't care. Yes it sucks when it feels like you are the only one hurting and he's running around with whomever. However, your jaded attitude is only sabotaging your own life, not his.

Doesn't matter how it happens – the wound requires time to mend. Most of the time, we whine about how it happened and when it happened to whomever will listen in the hopes of "figuring out" what *really* happened or uncovering some top secret keeping him from being "the one." Not likely. It didn't work. It's just over.

Breakup Sponsor

My suggestion for making it easier is ask one of your real friends to be your *Breakup Sponsor.* This friend serves many purposes, most of which is to keep you from doing anything stupid after a breakup. She can keep you on a recovery path versus a destructive one. I've heard 'em all... like calling him and hanging up multiple times. Or driving by his house. Or drunk dialing or drunk texting. Or showing up at his house with the false, hanging-by-a-thread hopes that seeing you will somehow change his mind. Or, even worse, showing up where he works. Ya, that'll make you popular.

Stop the madness and get yourself a sponsor. Even if you broke up with him, the pain you feel for hurting someone is unbelievable. It's far harder than you think it would be if you've never done it. If it's the right decision, get it over with and get support for yourself. Having someone help you doesn't mean you're a failure. It just means you aren't in it alone. Ask for help.

Tips for the Breakup Sponsor

Don't rush her through the process. It's brutal to watch someone you care for go through the pain and agony of a relationship ending. Rushing her through it or avoiding spending time with her so you don't have to watch isn't going to help. That's unbelievably selfish on your part.

She needs to feel the pain so she can heal through it instead of setting it aside and convincing herself she'll cope with it later. Well, later always comes and not usually when you'd like it to. Most likely, it'll be at the next date or the beginning of a potential relationship. Not such good timing for the emotional drama now magnified by denial or avoidance. So, help her take the time to heal when it happens.

She's grieving the loss of her relationship and will go through ups and downs. Don't let her dwell 24/7, though do listen when she needs to vent and be there when she needs to talk it out, or cry, or both. Then pick her up, get her in the shower and take her out to dinner, or to the park, or a ballgame or somewhere she feels at ease and positive energy surrounds her. No, I don't suggest taking her to a bar full of on-their-way-to-drunk men and artificial personality. That's just a *B.A.T.* nightmare waiting to happen. Go somewhere she can see that life continues and she's still a part of it.

You Get Dumped

When you get dumped it hurts like hell, particularly since it wasn't your idea. And especially if you thought things were going well and out of the blue, he's gone. You're stunned. Surprised. Blindsided even. Your heart was involved and you felt a connection with him… and you were sure he was the one. These feelings of despair, confusion and hurt are usually followed by us obsessing about the *way* he dumped us. Like if he'd done it differently it would feel better. Doesn't matter, you still got dumped.

Questioning Everything Since You Met

You may find yourself questioning everything you ever did since two seconds after you met Mr. Just Dumped Me. Ok, maybe one second. You dissect every single possibility to death wondering what you could've done differently, what you should've done differently... even to the point of questioning your outfits at various occasions.

WHOA!!!

You're Still Here

You are still very much alive and kickin'. Just because he chose to go on his merry way doesn't make you any less desirable. Just means you weren't someone he wanted in his life any longer. *Ouch* - I know. Sometimes, getting dumped is a big time clue YOU need to make different choices about who gets a chance.

The Heartbreak

Sometimes the heartbreak is because he really was a good guy, who met your *Deal Breakers*, and it didn't work out anyway. Most likely, because you didn't meet his. *Ouch* again. Well, that's assuming he actually knows what his *Deal Breakers* are.

Here's the reality – it doesn't matter whether he knows his *Deal Breakers* or *Must Haves* or has taken time to figure them out, he just dumped you so that's a pretty clear indicator you aren't "it" for him. That is a tough pill to swallow given you thought he was great for you, and he didn't reciprocate. From here, you can choose to be miserable, or you can choose to heal.

Being rejected isn't failing. Giving up is.

You Dump Him

This one is harder than it seems. If you care for this man and know he isn't the right one for you, be kind and end it. It isn't fair to string him along for your own selfish pleasure if he feels connected to you and you're pretty ambivalent about it. You wouldn't want a man to use you like that right? So why would you do it to him?

You'll Still Grieve

Be ready for the grieving period you're about to embark upon. It doesn't just apply to the scenario when you get dumped. Unless you are a heartless, calloused woman, you'll feel like crap about breaking his heart and will need to mourn the end of the relationship. Of course, if you had the mature conversation about expectations and what you want in a relationship, and you are both on the same page with that, breaking up shouldn't be such a big deal. Except, it always is. Emotions run high, pride is on the line, and egos are bruised. Nothing about that spells something pleasant.

Knowing Why - Our Need for "Closure"

Why do we seek the "final rejection" under the auspice of "closure?" It's like it isn't over yet. Even though he's stopped talking to you. Stopped calling... texting... emailing... smoke signals. Nothing. No communication whatsoever. Still - that isn't enough of a signal that it's over for us. We still need to have him tell us, straight up, that he's dumping us. The fact he's evaporated doesn't seem to be enough. What's up with that?

Seems there's a part of us who believes if he sees us again, he'll change his mind. Decide he can't actually live without us and we'll ride off into the sunset together. Hmmm… smacks of *Cinderella Head* justification. In reality, you're just choosing to persecute yourself further by insisting upon a verbal rejection, understanding "why" it ended and have a "solid" reason to cling to. Except there may not be one – at least one you will ever agree with.

What Just Happened?

Do I believe a breakup should actually be a conversation? Yes. Do I believe it is a mature way to end a relationship? Yes. Do I believe it's how a breakup should be handled every time? Yes, I do. Will it be the way it's handled with each man you date? Nope. At some point, you may meet *Mr. Vanishing Man B.A.T.* and will experience the wonder of "What just happened?" One minute we're together and happy, and the next he's gone.

You May Never Know Why

Sometimes there's isn't an answer to "Why?" Often if you're obsessing about knowing "why" you're assuming it's something about you. Something you did wrong or weren't good enough for. In reality, the expression "it's me, not you" may actually be true. So, it really may be him, not you.

A woman once shared with me that every time she gets dumped, she feels like a little piece of her heart dies. This was really early in her dating experience so she hadn't really felt this kind of rejection before. Not knowing why things ended was driving her crazy because she felt like she couldn't move forward without any "closure" for the situation. The bottom line is you may not get any.

Learning to provide some closure for yourself is an important step for your growth. And, as you learn more about relationships and making choices in dating, you'll discover breaking up doesn't break your heart forever. It's ok to be hurt and angry, it's also ok to be happy again.

It's a Two-Way Street

When it's you who wants to end things… step up, be the adult and have the conversation in person. Breaking up is a two way street and it doesn't have to be full of drama. Of course, having an adult face-to-face conversation about it really isn't going to make it feel any better, whether you are the one who wants out or not.

Most people have no interest in hurting another person, so if you are the one who is doing the breaking up – you are hurting someone. If you are the one being dumped… well that one is a little more obvious. Having an adult conversation about it is respectful of you and of him, and it's your choice if you are the one who is ending it. Could you call instead of seeing him? Yes, though that's only kinda being respectful and it's usually justified by saying it was better than text, email or just disappearing. Talk about a cop out. You wouldn't like him using that excuse so be careful of you using it.

Learn Something

There are lessons to be learned whether you dump him or he dumps you. *Always.* Could be the same lesson as last time if you keep choosing *Mr. Pattern B.A.T. Type* from the B.A.T. chapter. In that case, time to wake up. Hopefully, it's a new lesson to use when you try again this time.

Regardless, take the time to consider the lesson. Don't obsess about it and drive yourself and your friends bananas in the process, though do take some time to reflect and be grateful you have the insight to learn something from each experience. *Everyone gets rejected in life. It's how you respond, cope and heal that determines what will happen from here.*

A Journal Moment

You've really started to value yourself when you spend less time reacting to a breakup with "what's wrong with me" and more time learning something. Here are the three things you should learn with each experience: 1) something about yourself, 2) something from the experience of that relationship and that choice of man, and 3) a positive lesson you'll use *this time*.

Consider each relationship (could do this with dates too):

▸ What did you like about this man? What did you love? What did you respect?

▸ What didn't you like? What didn't you love? What didn't you respect?

▸ What did you appreciate about him?

- What worked well in the relationship? What didn't?

- What did he love, respect and appreciate about you? (No, don't ask him. Or use asking him as an excuse to contact him. Use your best judgment to answer the question. If you have no idea, that tells you something already. Your reaction to not knowing tells you something about your own needs.)

- What would you change? What would you stop doing?

- What did you learn about yourself through this experience?

- What's a positive lesson you can take with you to improve this time?

If all you have are negative lessons and a scowl, you're still in the hurt and angry phase of recovery and not ready to learn from the experience yet. When you're ready, dig a little deeper – there's something valuable in there somewhere.

Letting Go

You may find yourself hanging on even when he's already let go. I heard a story where a woman accidentally resent a text to a man who had broken up with her. His reply was "Who is this? Your number isn't in my phone." To say she felt stupid is an understatement. He clearly had let go, and she clearly was hanging on. I gently said, "Let it go. He doesn't care."

Delete and Disconnect

Purge your voice mail, email, and text messages, and disconnect from him in all social media. Even if you dumped him. Staying connected is hanging on. Watching his life happen without you isn't going to help your healing or ability to let go. Thinking he'll be hurt by watching yours is your desire for some sort of revenge from the pain he caused when he dumped you. It's not gonna matter, and it'll hurt you more than it'll hurt him.

The pictures of you two together usually provokes one extreme or the other – you want to rip them to shreds and burn them, or you want to hang onto them for your memories. Getting rid of them helps you let go. I didn't say it would be easy.

The Hardest Part

Hands down, letting go is the hardest part about a breakup. Getting through the pain, hurt and anger is no picnic, but letting go is so much harder. Here's why – if you truly let go - let the emotional connection go, let the friendship go if there was one, and let him go - you no longer have the breakup to obsess about. It's no longer serving as a protective shield against the next man, and the potential of being hurt again.

You may not have thought about it from this perspective before so here's another way to put it: Taking down the hurt and anger shield from the last man simultaneously shows your strength and puts you neck deep in your own vulnerability. It's a scary place. *Yet you can't truly open up to what might be coming until you let go of what's already gone.*

When you get to the point you can run into him in the grocery store and your hands don't start shaking, and you don't go hide in frozen foods, or you don't have a flash back to the pain of the breakup... you know you've let him go. Your reaction to running into him becomes more like "that's nice" without a second thought.

If You Have Kids Together

If you have kids together, letting go is a little more tricky. Obviously, you'll always be connected to him because he is their father, and you will still need to keep necessary photos and communicate with him for the kid's sake. Focus on what's needed to raise, care for and love your children, and do not put them in the middle of your divorce or breakup out of your own blinded hurt and anger. No trash talk about your ex, questioning your kids about his life or storming around and yelling about things he never did or wouldn't do for you that he is or isn't doing for someone else.

You know they didn't do anything to create the situation you are in, so don't unwittingly punish them for it. If you reacted strongly to me bringing up this point, it might be a little guilt talking because you may be doing what you know you shouldn't. Time to step back, work on healing yourself, and let go.

Release, Don't Avoid

The more you learn to heal and make a deliberate decision to move on, the more you will become focused on what you want instead of what you don't. Releasing and letting go is different than pushing from your mind. The first one acknowledges and embraces it happened then let's go, and the second avoids dealing with it. Avoiding just means it'll come back to haunt you later. Best to deal with it now and release it. You move toward what you choose to focus on so center on the good in your life right now, and the potential for the great things to come.

Is It Hanging On or Remembering?

Be aware of the difference between hanging on and remembering. You might find yourself in the remembering trap thinking you are recalling some pleasant things that happened with him, when in reality you are emotionally hanging onto him. Hanging on means you are still thinking about him, and some part of you still thinks there's a shot you'll get back together. Even when you know it's not good for you, and he didn't behave like he deserved you.

If you truly are remembering, you've moved past the emotional pain of hanging on and into the forgiveness of letting go. That includes forgiving him, and more importantly forgiving yourself for whatever role you had in the demise of your relationship. Remembering means you've acknowledged it's really over, learned something, and can even smile about the good times you had together. This is letting go.

When You're Wrong

One of the worst things about breaking up with someone, regardless of whose idea it was, is the feeling of being wrong about him. So wrong about what you thought you had together. So wrong about his nature, or his character, or that he really did care about you. You were wrong about him, and feel like a failure. You feel stupid because you believed in him and it didn't work like you thought it would -- leaving you to wonder, "Why didn't I see this coming?" *Sometimes getting it wrong is how you learn to get it right.*

Gotta Feel the Pain

Take the time to feel the pain. Trying to skip over the hurt, disappointment, confusion, missed connection, and generally feeling like dirt isn't going to help you heal. Staying stuck in this uneasy emotional state isn't healthy for you, though trying to skip it won't make you heal any faster. Honestly acknowledge the pain, and then let it go. As I said, stuffing it down and ignoring it most likely means it'll come back to haunt you sometime when you don't want it to. Continue to learn from your mistakes and keep going. Stuffing it down also makes you more guarded and less likely to be open to the next man who may be worthy of you.

I Wish It Were Different

You wish for something to be different... you wish you had known sooner... you wish it was different... But it's not. See him for who he really is, not who you want him to be. Take off the rose colored glasses and see the real man in front of you.

Work through the grief of what was, what you think you lost, and get to the place in your life of acceptance. You don't necessarily miss him. You may miss what you *thought he was* or what he would *become* in your life. Wishing it were different is a lot about giving up the dream of what you thought you had with him. *Know you can still have it with someone else.*

You're Getting Closer

As you work on you, each breakup is a step closer to the relationship you want. It's not what you want to hear after a breakup so give yourself time to be hurt and get angry. Then heal. If you're starting to see patterns in your choices, or determine you're choosing *B.A.T.s* for yourself, STOP IN YOUR TRACKS and regroup. It's time to choose a different path.

Accept the Reality

Accepting the reality of the breakup is a rocky road, though worth it for your own peace of mind and more importantly, for your *peace of heart*. For only after you reach *peace of heart* can you really move on again, without bitterness, resentment and without blaming the next guy for everything the last one did. This time, he could be your future so don't make him pay for the pains in your past.

Forgive Him and Yourself

Don't let the death of your relationship become the death of you and your life. One of the hardest parts is getting to this belief: "You're forgiven. I'm letting you go and I'm letting go of you." Remember to forgive yourself too so you're ready to welcome the possibilities ahead.

Let go of what was or could've been. Live in what is, and look toward what will come.

What Will You Choose?

Default	**Deliberate**
‣ Bitch to anyone who will listen.	‣ Use your *breakup anthem* and ask for help from your *breakup sponsor.*
‣ Hang on to being bitter, and live in the fear of being hurt again.	‣ Grieve, heal, accept it didn't work, let it go and forgive.
‣ Drag the vengeance from the last relationship into this one.	‣ Learn something to improve yourself.
‣ Keep wishing it were different.	‣ Choose to try again.

This Time

Use these affirming statements as encouragement when you need it or to celebrate deliberate changes you're making *this time.*

‣ *I know recovering from a breakup is a grieving process and will let myself feel the pain and heal.*

‣ *I will ask for help from my breakup sponsor and find an anthem that makes me feel alive.*

‣ *I accept it's over, stop trying to figure out why, truly let go, and learn something for this time.*

CHAPTER 10

The Possibilities

Taking the risk, and choosing a man worthy of you, puts you in a vulnerable position. You wonder if it will work out. Will you get hurt? Will he be the man he appears to be? You may feel weak, yet giving Mr. Contender a chance actually shows your true inner strength.

The best solution to this anxious, fragile quiver is *let it be a little uncomfortable.* Something new in life usually involves a little apprehension while we try to "figure out" how it might impact us. Well, in this case, figuring it out means you've been working on yourself, believe you are a catch, have defined *Mr. Right for You,* and commit to using your standards.

Give yourself permission to continue to stand in your own power and make choices that honor you. The more you believe you can cope with the pain if it doesn't work out and know you'll still be ok, and have the faith that it could work out, the more centered you'll feel.

It's easy to say when you are sitting on your couch reading this book. The real test is when you apply what you learned to your life, dates and relationships. You can do this.

There Are Men Everywhere

Stay open to the possibilities, live your life and put yourself in situations where you may meet him. Choose to spend time doing things you enjoy where you may meet someone who shares your interests. You might find a man who meets your *Deal Breakers* and *Must Haves*, and likes some things you do. Think of it as creating your own opportunities. Other options are online dating, a dating service or blind dates through your friends.

There are literally men everywhere… are any of them *Mr. Right for You*? Who knows? When you take charge of your life, including your dating life, and make deliberate decisions that honor you, the world opens up with opportunity.

Embrace this feeling and remember it on those days when you may be heart broken or disappointed by someone. Keep *possibility* in your heart, your mind, and your soul. As I've said before, you see what you look for so focus on all the good men in the world, and you'll start to notice they are around you. You're right, some of them are married or gay… but not all of them. The clearer you are on what you want, the easier it will be to weed out the men who don't meet your standards and recognize *Mr. Right for You* when he appears.

Use Your Head *and* Your Heart

You are on the right track of choosing someone worthy when you are ready to look beyond the superficial stuff and consider his character, soul and beliefs. No man is perfect and neither are you. This is about choosing someone who deserves you and who you like. Not just love.

You have to *like* him and want to spend time around him. Liking him comes from your head, loving him comes from your heart.

The *feelings* in your heart speak to the chemistry between you and the budding connection. That's only one part of *Choosing Who Gets a Chance*. The purpose of a standards list is to *make sense of your heart* - meaning what your head is telling you about his character, how he treats you now and how he'll treat you later. So if you need him, will he be there for you or at a ballgame he wouldn't think of leaving?

Making decisions with your head and your heart means you're choosing with common sense from your head and the feelings from your heart.

Heartbreak is Part of Life

The fastest route to staying single is being afraid of getting hurt. Accepting the fact it may not work out is part of dating success. I don't mean accepting it intellectually and understanding it in your head. That's the easy part. The true success is accepting it in your heart and soul and believing it's just a part of life.

Guess that's another thing people won't tell you. This time it's not because they don't know… it's because they do. No one wants to say it won't work out. I don't either. I'd much rather focus on the positive things in life and direct my energy on the good.

Possibility of Success

Until you accept it may not work out, the fear is winning. When you accept it, and make a deliberate decision to *try anyway* – you are honoring yourself by believing in your own choices and having the confidence to deal with whatever happens from here. It shows you trust your own judgment, and if you are wrong, you are strong enough to handle it. The pain from being wrong beats the regret of not trying. *Now, you are open to the possibility of success instead of living in the petrified fear of failure.*

Finding Mr. Right *for You*

I've heard this many times, "The complicated part is finding him." I take that a step further to clarify a few things because it doesn't mean finding Mr. Perfect. And, it's not finding Mr. Right *according to everyone else.* Nor is it finding Mr. Good Enough. *It's finding Mr. Right for You.* And, knowing when you have.

Of course, the two keys you've found him are he meets your criteria, from your head and your heart, and *you meet his.* It's always a mutual thing. He could be who you think is *Mr. Right for You,* yet if you aren't *Ms. Right for Him…* it's a swing and a miss. You may have thought he was right, but *he's only right if you mean to him the same as he means to you, and you both want the same kind of relationship.*

There's a big difference between having a crush, lusting after him, liking him, and truly being in love. You'll figure out the difference as you choose a man to date, stay true to yourself and your *Deal Breakers,* and experience a relationship with him.

As you gain more experience, your standards and choices of who is good for you may change, though you will still have them. Especially since you're becoming more comfortable with yourself "in your own skin" as the expression goes, and learning more about what you want. You'll also learn about each other's flaws, and if they are the kind where you can appreciate each other anyway. He's human and imperfect, and so are you.

Dating Fatigue

Keeping the faith of the possibilities is sometimes the hardest part. You'll likely have moments of doubt, feel like you're spinning your wheels and wonder if you should stick to your standards because "he just isn't out there." It might even mean you'll repeat patterns and choose *B.A.T.s* to date.

Dating fatigue feels especially heavy when you've done the work on yourself, defined your *Deal Breakers* and figured out what you want... and he still hasn't shown up yet. One crucial question: Did you actually do the work on yourself or just read the info and think, "Ya... Ya... I get it." Take time to reflect upon your beliefs and who you are before you jump by that part. It's crucial to being your true self and choosing a good man you deserve.

Take a Break

When you feel yourself wavering, questioning and wondering if it's all worth it – take a break from dating. Gazing in your closet and sighing at the thought of picking out another first date outfit, knowing the menu at your favorite meeting spot better than the servers, and wishing for a recording of your favorite childhood story because you are tired of telling it are all signals it's time for a break. You've stopped having fun on your dating journey and are starting to loathe the process.

Just recognize the reason why you're taking a break. Is it a break because you are hiding or because you aren't quite over someone or because you're exhausted and really need a time out? It's your life to live and you decide if you want to date, have a relationship, or be single.

Taking the Risk

As you continue your dating and relationship journey, there will always be lessons to learn. Even after *Mr. Right for You* has arrived. At some point, if you continue to remember *The Secret - It Starts With You*, you'll reach a place of inner peace for yourself. The kind where you know what's important to you, what you want, what you're willing to compromise on, and make deliberate decisions for yourself. *When you're smart about your choices and know your priorities, it's easier to choose the risk.*

Let It Be Simple

Choose a man who is looking for the same type of relationship you are. If he wants something casual and you don't, it'll be a bumpy road while you or he tries to convince the other one to change or you'll both just ignore the facts and "hope for the best." Or, it'll just end. Accept where he is and what he wants and choose someone who wants what you do.

Be truthful about your intentions, especially with yourself. Having the confidence to communicate where you are in life and what you are looking for says, "I'm comfortable with myself and my life." If you're looking for something with the potential to become serious, admit that to yourself, and then be ok with the consequences if he isn't looking for the same thing. This is about timing, not judgment. Have the confidence to move on and try again. When you let it be that simple, the whole process is less stressful.

Be Careful of the Critics

When you discover a man who has potential, ask yourself if the things you appreciate about him are the right reasons for you to keep him? "Right" meaning right for you. Be careful of the critics who say you just can't commit if you won't stay with this "nice guy." Just because what others see makes this man *Look Good On Paper* doesn't mean he's the right man for you. They aren't experiencing how he lives his life and how he treats you. This is your life and your decision to make.

If He's a Contender

If he is a contender for *Mr. Right for You*, it takes courage to stay in it and choose the risk. You found what you said you wanted, so you owe it to yourself to give it a chance. Stick to your guns so to speak and make the decision that's true for you. I'm not going to say you'll live happily ever after. That's a *Cinderella Head* myth given it implies it just magically happens. Only you and *Mr. Right for You* can make the continuous effort to create it, whatever that means for both of you.

If he isn't the one, give yourself permission to use your strength and breakup with him. I've heard from countless people who *settled* and married the one who was in front of them. Now they are divorced, or worse yet, still married and miserable. How is that better than being single?

Someone Better

When you've found someone, be careful of thinking you can't stop with him because "someone better" must be out there. This might be your "creep radar" on overload, or nit-picking about little things that don't actually bother you but have become a defense mechanism. Don't expect that he'll never make mistakes or do something that bugs you. Keep in mind you already learned he meets your *Deal Breakers* and has the qualities you wrote on your *Mr. Right for You* list.

Know when you're just being chicken at the idea of taking the risk, and you're getting antsy assuming the grass must be greener. You might also be thinking since you found what you wanted you have something to lose. This is the vulnerability and fear steering your path, not you. The upside is you value him enough that it matters, and my hope for you is the feeling is mutual from him.

Will Your Deliberate Decisions Always Be Right?

Making *deliberate* decisions isn't about being right or wrong - it's about how you make the decisions, and how you feel about the ones you've made. Doesn't mean you know everything, and doesn't mean you ever will. It means you are making *good* decisions for yourself because they are based on what you know at the time, what you've learned about yourself and from the perspectives of your *real friends*, and from your own experience.

If you've worked on you, figured out what's important and have stuck to your standards, the choices you make in your love life now come from a source of *trust within yourself*. The odds are good those decisions will be better for you, though it's not a guarantee they will be "right." Things still may not work out the way you want, and mistakes will still happen. It's just part of life and being human. Because you owned your choice and made it from a source of trust, you know you can cope with whatever happens, learn from it and move on.

Being deliberate will also change how you make decisions in other areas of your life, and how you feel about the ones you've made. Does it mean you're now perfect? No. It does mean you feel centered and strong enough to live in your own power. *You'll be more at ease with not knowing what will happen next, and more comfortable with letting your life evolve.*

A Journal Moment

Consider times in your life when you took a risk and it worked out.

Consider a time when it didn't.

‣ What did you learn about yourself from each experience?

‣ How can you use that knowledge in relationships?

‣ What can you be more deliberate about right now?

Relationships Take "Work"

I've never liked this expression. Yes, relationships take effort, though "work" is generally perceived as something negative. If you don't want to make an effort, or put some "work" into it, then accept you won't develop good relationships. You can choose to stay single. If you want someone to share your life with, then expect a requirement to make an effort and pay attention to him. Of course, this is always a two way street. If you are making an effort, and he isn't, no deal. Or, if he's making an effort, and you aren't, then he may decide no deal.

What Are You Working At?

Something else to consider is what are you working at? If you meet each other's *Deal Breakers*, each have the character and values desired, and want the same type of relationship, you have a great start. Learning about each other's needs and how to meet them evolves as you continue to get to know each other. Is it always easy? Of course not. It requires consistent and genuine attention to each other and your relationship.

Just as business relationships require ongoing attention and nurturing to be truly engaging and productive, so do personal ones. Some of you have more experience with this than others, and some of you have been married before so you have first hand experience of how this has worked in your past love life.

Just be careful not to project your last date, marriage, live in, or long-term relationship onto this one. You are different now and you have chosen a man worthy of you. You both deserve a clean slate and the opportunity to make your own rules.

Communication Makes or Breaks Your Relationship

Communication is the make or break element of any relationship - personal, professional, business, family, romantic, friendship or any other form. I'd take it one step further and say communication is the method, though understanding is what you're really seeking, and the whole process to create it is fraught with potential for misfires.

Misfires at Work

Consider how much time you spend at work managing misfires created by communication attempts that didn't work. Each communication method has its own built in issues and potential for misunderstandings: email, voice mail, text, phone calls, and video conference. Even in a face to face conversation we may not get it right. Someone might still say, "That's not what I said" or "That's not what I meant" or "You're taking it the wrong way" or "There seems to be a misunderstanding" or "We're not on the same page about this."

Misfires in Your Love Life

The same opportunity for misfires happens in your personal relationships, and dating life, and may even create similar responses. Truly seeking mutual understanding takes more effort than the act of communicating, because without it all you did was talk, or send an email or leave a message or give a look. Or, all you did was think you listened, yet the intended message from the other person didn't get through.

Mutual Understanding Doesn't Mean You Agree

I didn't say mutual understanding always means you agree on everything. Just that both people want to make the effort to create it. Once you're there, you can choose to agree to disagree and respect each other's perspective or beliefs. Or, you can decide if the relationship is working, and make some deliberate decisions to change, improve or end it.

Communication Keeps It Alive

If the relationship is working, communication is what keeps it alive and helps it evolve. It seems when people talk about intimacy, they are usually referring to sex. To me, intimacy is a mutual emotional connection with the comfort to be vulnerable. If the relationship continues this far, it could mean unconditional love. *Communication is how it starts and how it grows.*

If It's Serious

If your relationship is getting serious, I'd suggest conversations about religion/spirituality, children, living situation (dishes, laundry, house cleaning etc.), living location, money philosophy - like if it's shared or separate, spending and saving habits, current debt, investments, credit scores, what you see later in life for you as individuals and as a couple, and paying the bills for starters. If you're serious, you've already been through your *Deal Breakers* and experienced if he's a man you believe is a good match for you. Be sure you address the business of life too.

If you don't want to talk about it before you get married, why do you expect to talk about it after? If you don't want to potentially rock the boat before you walk down the aisle, you certainly won't want to afterwards. Avoiding these topics doesn't make them go away, and if you live together or get married, side stepping them could create dire consequences given you're now tied together.

If it feels too early for these topics, maybe it's not getting serious yet. Over time, these subjects will come up as you share on a deeper level. If you're avoiding the business of life, it could mean you haven't built the connection for these to be comfortable conversations yet, or it could mean one of you is more serious about the relationship than the other.

Men's Potato Chip Ego

One specific note about communication - when you discover a man worthy of a chance with you, be conscientious of his ego. It's fragile, like a potato chip. It's not just my experience speaking, its input from men telling me this is important for women to understand.

Some men's sense of values and character may be stronger than steel, yet his need to be appreciated by you is crucial to his sense of self-worth. Yes, I could go on and on about him defining his own self-worth separate from you, but that is distinct from the worth he derives from your appreciation. In a real relationship, most men need their women to notice the things they do. And, they need us to do something to show our appreciation. He wants to know you are proud of him so be sure you tell him and show him. *Just like you want to know he's proud of you and appreciates what you do for him.*

The Heart of the Matter

Deliberate decisions that are good for you.

1. Recognize your *dating age*, choose to do things differently, and start down the path of *Living Deliberately*.

2. Let go of the romantic delusions in your *Cinderella Head* and stop tolerating ridiculous behavior from the men you date. Understand your expectations and values about *sex* and how long you want to wait before you have it. Know what makes a *friends with benefits* scenario and if it is or isn't right for you.

3. Seek out your *real friends*, love your *broken friends*, and laugh with your *cheering friends*. Have the courage to ask for your real friends' honest perspective instead of just commiserating with your other friends. Be smart about safety and ask them to make the *security call* during your date.

4. Know why understanding *drama* is important, its silent damage to your love life, its source, and how your *Drama Queen* tendencies show up in the *Drama Queen Types*. Vow to live differently.

5. Wherever you are starting, be the *Leading Lady* who understands you are single, not alone. Take charge of your life, and live from your own power. You've healed from your past, stopped compromising your present, embraced what's important to you, and have fun being the *best version of yourself.*

6. Consider the *B.A.T. Signs* and *B.A.T. Types* and think carefully before you choose to date one. Don't try to create what you want with a man who is the wrong choice - *Not every man deserves a chance with you.*

7. Don't define what you want by what you have or what you find. Discover your *Deal Breakers, Must Haves* and *Nice to Haves,* learn *Basic Facts* along the way, and *choose* a man with potential for *Mr. Right for You.* You know *Love is Blind Only if You Are.*

8. Even when you feel exhausted, lonely and frustrated in the *dating burnout trap... do not settle* for *Mr. Good Enough* or *Mr. He'll Do.* Face the truth of *you're about to settle danger signs* — believe you deserve better and end it. When you've chosen well, settling can mean avoiding the man who gives you butterflies in your stomach because you're too scared to find out if he feels the same. To have a relationship, you'll have to trust someone at some point.

9. Accept *breaking up* as part of dating. Stop obsessing about why it ended; heal, learn, let go, forgive and look ahead. When it's you who wants to end it, have the courage to say so. Ask your *breakup sponsor* for help and play your *anthem* when you need it.

10. Be open to the *possibilities,* truly live in your own *power, trust* yourself, and *take charge of your life.* Believe it's ok to *take a break* from dating when you need it or simply *enjoy being single.* When you find a contender for *Mr. Right for You* - know his life issues and share yours, choose to take the risk, make the effort, understand *communication* makes or breaks

your relationship, and *make good deliberate decisions with your head and your heart.*

As you continue to learn about yourself, be patient. There will be days when you wish you knew it all right this minute. You know life doesn't work that way, and certainly not in relationships. Each interaction with someone is an opportunity to learn something new, about them and about you.

With each stage of this journey, your confidence and strength help you recognize the magnificent woman you already are, and choose to become. Starting with yourself, developing your standards, and having the courage to use them, connects what you need with what you want and who you choose. Looking ahead, it all comes together to increase the chances of finding *Mr. Right for You.*

CONTACT THE AUTHOR

Learn more about Debra Kunz:

www.debrakunz.com

Join dating conversations:

www.deliberatedating.com

Share a book review:

www.amazon.com

www.barnesandnoble.com

www.goodreads.com

www.shelfari.com

Request a workshop, book signing, or ask Debra to speak for your group:

info@debrakunz.com

To purchase bulk copies of *Love is Blind Only if You Are*:

info@debrakunz.com

GLOSSARY

Basic Facts – List of things to learn about him that will help you understand his history, his life now, and where he's going.

B.A.T. – A man who is **B**ad **A**ss **T**rouble from the beginning, yet you make excuse after excuse to justify why you are still dating him. There are several signs and types of **B**ad **A**ss **T**rouble.

B.A.T. Sign – Indicators of **B**ad **A**ss **T**rouble.
    Drinks Too Much – This B.A.T. Sign is related to your own drinking habits and attitude about what's social versus what's partying, and your acceptance of each. It's also influenced by your Dating Age (and his) and if you are re-living your party years, never got to have them, or they just continued.

    Flashes Money – He may have money to throw around, and stories about his spending, though can he talk about anything else? You should wonder if he has any depth of character to go with his riches.

    He Cheated in Prior Relationships – It'll make you question if you can trust him. Listen to his story and decide for yourself. Have the strength to walk away if the answer that comes to you is no.

He Doesn't Know What He Wants from a Woman – This statement means he's still learning about himself and what he values. Decide whether or not you want to be his tutor because he may take his new knowledge on the road, and not with you.

He Drives by the Ex's House with You in the Car – He's still stuck on the ex, living in the past, or hasn't let go of his last breakup.

He Knows How to be Arrested – This one simply makes me say "Yikes!"

How He Communicates – B.A.T. Sign where you need to understand your own communication needs, if his style meets them, if you are willing to understand his style, and if he's willing to understand yours.

Inconsistencies – What he says and what he does don't match; for instance he claims he's a family man yet doesn't make time for his kids.

Never Met His Friends, Doesn't Want to Meet Yours – He keeps you from your friends, or won't introduce you to his. Most likely, he's not very interested in you or he's hiding something.

No Room for Compromise – He's controlling, always right, doesn't want to hear what you have to say, or anything about your perspective. His opinion is the only one that matters.

Only Calls at the Last Minute – You aren't a priority.

Only Compliments Your Physical Appearance – His desire for sex with you is clear, though most likely he has no desire for you otherwise.

Only Talks About Himself – A self-centered man with expectations of being taken care of. Your needs won't matter.

Promises The Future Way Too Soon – There are three options with this one: 1) the insecure man who's afraid to be alone and finds you an attractive distraction rather than someone he actually chooses to be part of his life; 2) the lazy man who doesn't want to do housework and sees you as a good substitute; 3) the man who actually has his act together, has done some work on his emotional issues, and truly values you in his life. Your gut knows which one it is, not your Cinderella Head.

Something Doesn't Add Up – The little voice inside your head is asking "What's up with this guy?" If that's not enough, listen to the knots in your stomach, and your uneasy feeling each time you have a conversation with him.

Your Friends Vanish – Your friends get tired of you choosing so far below your standards that they stop spending time with you and the man you are dating.

Your Physical Reaction – Your gut's in knots and you know it isn't because you are nervous, it's because he's creepy.

B.A.T. Type – Different kinds of **B**ad **A**ss **T**rouble based on their situation and/or character, or more likely lack of character.

Drunk B.A.T.s Can't Dance – You met this B.A.T. Type when he was drunk, and maybe you were too. He's not himself when he's drunk, and neither are you, so be sure you spend time together when you're both sober so you can learn some real things about each other. If being drunk is a chronic condition, it could be a serious issue and it'll mess up your life rhythm, not just your rhythm on the dance floor.

He's Not Interested – He doesn't initiate any contact, yet you are still convincing yourself he's interested in you. Late night Booty Calls don't count as genuine interest.

Just Divorced – Special kind of Mr. Project B.A.T. Type. The aftermath of his failed marriage results in an emotionally broken state. Most likely, he doesn't know how broken he is so your job is to make good decisions for yourself.

Looks Good on Paper Man – Using your written list, this B.A.T. Type appears to meet your Must Haves and Deal Breakers. However, you won't know if he's worthy beyond "on paper" until you meet him, feel the chemistry, see how he lives his life, experience his character, and how he treats you.

Mamma's Boy – He's a little too attached to his mother and has a triple twist: 1) he lives with his parents with no apparent need for his presence in their home, 2) his parents enable him to live there instead of teaching him to become an independent man, 3) Mamma has a power trip over his life and he doesn't recognize it. With this B.A.T. you'll find a man who expects to be taken care of, not a man who wants to be your partner in life.

MEGA B.A.T. – This B.A.T. Type is the ultimate trouble, and probably combines all the B.A.T. Signs and maybe even some of the other B.A.T. Types. He's full of ego, thinks he walks on water, and pays attention to you only when it's convenient for him. The biggest problem is you're still convincing yourself he actually cares about you.

Mr. Project – He is an emotional mess, stuck in the past, and blames everyone else for the problems in his life yet hasn't done any work on himself to address his role in how his life has turned out. Ms. Fix It Drama Queen is drawn to Mr. Project B.A.T. like a moth to a flame.

Mr. Separated – This man isn't single and available to choose you, he's still married. It isn't over 'till it's over and his complicated life begs the question, "Is he working on his marriage or working on his exit plan?" Either way, there's nothing there for you.

Pattern Man – This type is about you and your relentless choice to date, commit to, or marry the same kind of man, most likely a B.A.T., while hoping each time for different results.

Vanishing Man – You don't know about him until after he's gone. One day you are together and the next he disappeared, leaving you to wonder "what just happened?"

Best Version of Yourself – Knowing how great you are today, and always evolving to become even better.

B.I.T.C.H. – A man's term "Babe In Total Conflict With Herself" used to illustrate the inconsistency between what a woman says she wants, the choices she makes, and how she chooses to behave. This acronym describes a woman who struggles with the Girl and Woman Within issues.

Bitter or Better – Choosing to learn something from a breakup and becoming better for it, or choosing to blame him, hold onto the pain, and remain bitter.

Booty Call – Contact from a man who only wants sex. Usually happens late at night though not always.

Break the Pattern – When you stop Compromising Yourself and what you want, and start making relationship decisions that truly reflect all the love and devotion you deserve.

Breakthrough Epiphany – The moment you recognize that you are the common denominator of the problems or successes in your love life, and choose to do something to change it this time.

Breakup – An unfortunate reality of dating, otherwise we'd just marry whomever we met first. Could be you got dumped or you dumped him. Either way, it ended and you'll grieve the loss.

Breakup Anthem – Song you play for yourself to lift your spirits and make you smile while recovering from a breakup.

Breakup Lesson – Examining your breakup from a more objective perspective, and discovering something about yourself and your choices you can use this time. The lessons learned are usually discovered after you've coped with the emotional pain, frustration, hurt and anger of the loss.

Breakup Sponsor – Friend who helps you recover from a breakup and keeps you from doing stupid things in your highly vulnerable, emotional state.

Broken Friend – Friend who cares for you, but is going through her (or his) own life changes and problems, and could drag you down into the muck with them. Love them where they are, and don't let them hold you back.

Cheering Friend – Friend who is supportive and wants you to get what want, though won't tell you what you need to hear for fear of creating a conflict. In contrast, Real Friends tell you the truth.

Chemistry – The glint in your eye, shortness of breath, or butterflies in your stomach when you look at him, talk or touch. It's a heart emotion with not much common sense or logic. There are several types based on his vibe or your reaction to him.

Chemistry Types Based on His Vibe

Blend Chemistry – A combination of some strong, take charge traits of Manly Man Vibe Chemistry with the perceptive, thoughtful traits of Sensitive Man Vibe Chemistry.

Manly Man, Man's Man Chemistry – Masculine, strong, protective and take charge. "Strong, silent type" might be the stereotype.

Refined Chemistry – He's a gentleman with some sophisticated interests, and you have no worries about how he'll act when you're in public together.

Rough Around the Edges Chemistry – He's definitely a "guy" who needs some training, plus you aren't quite sure how he'll behave in public. Guess that's only an issue if it matters to you.

Sensitive Man Chemistry – Perceptive, understanding, and listens to your every word. He's probably protective and strong, though it's not as obvious as with Manly Man Chemistry.

Chemistry Types Based on Your Reaction to Him

Friend Chemistry – You feel good around him, except there's no spark.

Intrigue Chemistry – This might be a disguise for something interesting only to learn it's the bad boy B.A.T. attraction.

None – Enough said.

Rip Each Other's Clothes Off Chemistry – This man is smokin' hot and smoldering. At its core, this is lust.

Spark of Desire Chemistry – There's interest plus a spark of attraction because you might have found the man you are looking for using your Mr. Right for You standards.

Choose Him – The belief that we choose the man we want, not take whatever we can get.

Cinderella Head – Few women escape the society programming that begins in childhood and teaches us to believe that whatever man shows up must be the one we're supposed to be with, even though he doesn't give you what you need, or lives a life you want to blend with your own. You do whatever it takes to make him like you, and then wait for him to commit, while justifying his ridiculous behavior because "He's a man and that's just how they are." It doesn't cross your mind you could choose a different man for yourself.

Communication Misfires – Lack of mutual understanding which can make or break relationships of all types: personal, professional, romantic, family, friends, marriage, and kids.

Compromising Yourself – Allowing yourself to ignore what you really want by losing yourself to other's expectations, denying you aren't happy, letting your "smart women's pride" make your decisions, or choosing a man based on his acceptance of what you think is wrong with you instead of expecting him to partner with the whole you.

Critics – People who will want you to lower your standards and settle.

Danger Signs of Settling – There are several signs and excuses used to justify keeping the man who is in front of you. Excuses: the length of time you've been together, your biological clock, he's a good man even though you know he isn't the right man for you, or simply the convenience of the relationship. Signs: you don't actually like, love, trust or respect him, he doesn't live a lifestyle you want, or you toss aside your standards list and let your Cinderella Head take over.

Date or Relationship – Date is a short get together like dinner, lunch or a drink without automatic expectations of another one. Relationship means you are mutually invested in each other beyond just enjoying time together at the moment.

Date Repellant – Oozing desperation or showering it all over him.

Dating Age – This age has nothing to do with the year you were born, and everything to do with your degree of comfort, experience, understanding, and knowledge about dating.

Dating Break – Deciding to take yourself off the dating market for awhile. Might be because of Dating Fatigue, or it could be to recover from a breakup.

Dating Burnout – Beyond Dating Fatigue into flat out, "I'm staying home and never want to date again." There's danger you'll settle for the man you're with now because you don't want to date anymore.

Dating Fatigue – You've been dating so long, or so often lately, you wish you had your favorite childhood story on tape. It's especially exhausting when you've done the work on yourself, know your standards, are using them, and just haven't met the right man yet. Careful, this is on the road to Settling.

Deal Breaker – A list of about five items discovered during the What Do You Know About Him Process. If he has one or more of them, you'll automatically pass on dating him.

Default Dating Cycle – Dating pattern where you stay stuck in the "there are no good men left" attitude, choose B.A.T.s to date, and continue to complain that "men are jerks," without looking at your contributions to the problems in your love life. It's a continuous loop until you have the Breakthrough Epiphany and realize you are the common denominator to the problems or successes in your love life.

Default Living – Blindly living your life on autopilot without regard for what you really want.

Deliberate Dating – First: know yourself, understand your needs and what you want. Second: decide your standards for Mr. Right for You, have the courage to use them, and choose accordingly.

Deliberate Decisions – Decisions made through knowing yourself, trusting your choices, and believing in your ability to embrace the outcome. They include the wisdom from your head and the emotions from your heart.

Deliberate Living – Living on purpose after taking time to understand yourself and what's truly important to you, taking charge of your life, and choosing how you want to live, who you want in your life, and why.

Doormat – Let others walk all over you, never say no to people even when you want to, and worry about being liked. You definitely aren't living in your own power and likely choosing B.A.T.s to date.

Drama Queen – A woman who lives for chaos in her life and seeks it out or creates more – especially when there isn't enough upheaval happening on its own. Her insecurity and need for validation drives life's decisions and damages her love life. The types are listed below.

> **He's All I Can Get** – The belief you aren't good enough for a good man, so you settle for whoever shows up. Low self-esteem drives your choices and makes this type an easy target for a MEGA B.A.T.

> **Ms. Fix It** – Your need to be needed drives your life so you choose men who have lots of drama to fix. The more broken he is, the more you are drawn to him. Mr. Project B.A.T. is catnip for this Drama Queen.

> **Stirring Things Up** – When you get bored, or life is too easy, you create some chaos in your relationship so your man has to do something to reassure you he'll stay. Otherwise, this Drama Queen constantly fears he'll leave because there's nothing going on where he has to prove he still cares.

> **The Chip on Your Shoulder** – You're scared of getting hurt and use your bitter, jaded attitude as a brick wall around you, just daring a man to knock it down and prove he's worthy. The good men will keep walking because they know you're a mess; the B.A.T.s may stop by and take on the challenge of the chase, though not with the intention of sticking around.

> **Your Baggage is Showing** – You are manipulative, keep secrets and are generally bitchy all because your Emotional

Clutter is wide and deep. You expect the men in your life to manage your issues instead of dealing with your past and managing yourself.

Drama Source – The root of a Drama Queen's unaware need for chaos is her internal emotional turmoil, insecurity and need for validation.

Emotional Clutter – Hoarding or holding onto emotional damage from your past life, relationship and dating experiences.

Face the Truth – When you pay attention to all the danger signs of settling, and acknowledge the man you're with isn't the one for you.

Friends with Benefits (FWB) – A mutually established sexual relationship without expectations of dating or monogamy.

Girl and Woman Within – Beliefs we've absorbed about dating and relationships throughout our life, and the conflict that may be created from the romantic and less self aware version of what we want (girl), versus the more mature version of what we choose (woman). Men have a name for this - B.I.T.C.H. "Babe In Total Conflict With Herself."

Giving Up Friends – The unfortunate situation created by the end of a long-term relationship or marriage where friends may choose to "take sides," or you may choose to do it for them.

Hanging On or Remembering – After a breakup, this is the distinction between remembering good times you had together, or emotionally hanging onto those memories as a way to stay tied to him.

Head and Heart Decisions – Decisions made using both the common sense from your head and the feelings from your heart.

"He's Different" Syndrome – The justification for dating a man who is clearly a B.A.T. by blindly ignoring the signs and types he shows you, or convincing yourself that he'll change his wayward behavior for you. You're most likely thinking with your Cinderella Head.

I Don't Want To Scare Him Off – If he's interested in you or wants to be in a relationship with you, he won't be scared. If he is, it could be your values don't match, you don't have the same expectations about a relationship, or it's an issue with him, not with you. Unless, you do ridiculous things like drive by his house constantly, call him numerous times a day, or other stalker-like behaviors that would scare anyone off.

If He Calls or Not – Decision point where you can freak out because he didn't call and assume there's something wrong with you, or choose to live from your own power and make a choice whether or not he gets another chance.

I Wish It Were Different – After a breakup you fantasize about how you thought it would work out and still hold onto the hope it will. Accept it isn't, and let it go.

Knowing Why, Breakup – Our need to understand why we just got dumped using the cover of "closure," while in reality we're wondering what's wrong with us that made him decide to breakup. It's related to the Questioning Everything Since You Met phenomenon where we dissect every conversation and everything we ever did together hoping to figure out why it ended.

Leading Lady – Empowered woman who lives and enjoys her life on her own terms. You listen to others' input and ideas, though you make your own decisions and feel good about it. Becoming a Leading Lady means you've taken charge of your life, without trying to control it.

Letting Go – This is a crucial part of coping with a breakup where you let go of him, who you thought he was or would become in your life. You can't truly be open to new possibilities until you let go of what's already gone.

Live Your Standards – Establishing your standards, giving yourself permission to use them, and having the courage to actually do so.

Love is Blind Only if You Are – You aren't blind when you take the time to learn about yourself, understand what you need, and define what you want - before you decide who he should be. Evaluate the B.A.T. risk, get comfortable with weeding out the men who don't meet your standards, and make decisions that honor you.

Mr. Contender – This man has potential to be Mr. Right for You and you know it. It's scary because giving him a chance puts you neck deep in your own vulnerability, yet taking the risk on a man worthy of you really shows your true strength.

Mr. Right for You – The man you've chosen based first on knowing yourself and understanding your needs and then defining what you want and why you want it using the What Do You Know About Him Process.

Must Have – A list of essential characteristics for Mr. Right for You as determined in the What Do You Know About Him Process.

Nice to Have – A list of bonus characteristics that aren't required for Mr. Right for You as determined in the What Do You Know About Him Process.

No Standards – You settle for what you can get instead of believing you deserve someone great. You accept every man who crosses your path because you don't know the difference between who shows up and what you want.

Not Every Man Deserves A Chance – Recognizing that not every man you meet deserves a chance with you.

Peace of Heart – Occurs when you have recovered from a breakup, discovered the lessons you can use this time, and let go of the pain, hurt, anger and frustration. True peace of heart includes forgiving him and yourself.

Personal Power – Knowing and believing you are worthy of love and devotion, and feeling centered within yourself and your life, without influence from others.

Picky – Dating criteria used by a guarded, scared woman who wants a man in her life, yet her unrealistic standards become a barrier to choosing one given no man will ever measure up. Others may use this word because they don't know the difference between Picky and Selective - you do.

Potato Chip Ego – Illustration for how fragile a man's ego can be, and their need for the women in their lives to tell and show them we appreciate the things they do for us.

Questioning Everything Since You Met – Breakup stage where you dissect every conversation and everything you ever did together hoping to figure out why it ended. Mostly this just makes you cry harder because there aren't any answers.

Real Friend – Friend who cares for you and gives an honest perspective on your dating (and life) decisions, especially when you are caught up in the emotions of a situation like dating a B.A.T.

Relating Age – Your comfort, knowledge, experience and understanding about how to connect with others and build relationships of all types.

Relationship Goggles – Wearing relationship goggles means you're blaming the next guy for what the last one did, and measuring the next relationship based on the past. It's not fair to him or to you.

Relationships Take Work – Any type of relationship takes effort, though defining what you are working at is a key step. If you don't want to make a deliberate effort to build the loving relationship you seek, then stay single.

Security Call – Planned call from a friend during the first 30-45 minutes of a date to verify you are safe.

Selective – Deliberate choices about the men you date based on your Mr. Right for You standards. Not the same as picky.

Settle – Dating, committing to, or marrying a man who doesn't give you what you need, or live a life you want to become part of, or that you may not even like, love or trust, but is a substitute for being alone.

Settling Danger Zone and Settling Trap – Letting that lonely feeling make your decisions as you consider keeping the man you are dating, whether or not he meets your standards. If you were asked about him you'd shrug and say, "He'll do."

Sex: Values, Behavior and Expectations – Take time to understand your values about having sex while dating and having sex during a relationship. Be sure what you want and how you behave matches. If you want a relationship, discuss mutual expectations about what sex means to you and to him before you hop in the sac.

Single, Not Alone – Acknowledging the life status of being single simply means you aren't married. It doesn't mean you are alone in your life - you have friends, family, colleagues, pets, neighbors and others.

Taking the Risk – The courage you need to give a man who is a contender for Mr. Right for You the chance he deserves. It's after you learn about yourself first, understand what you need, define and use your standards, and evaluate the B.A.T. risk.

That **Dating Place** – Having a desire to date, but aren't sure how to go about it or if it could be easier, plus the concern "if you're doing it right." It usually includes the questions, "Is he interested?" and "How do I know?"

The Secret – Discovering all good relationships begin with understanding yourself, being happy with yourself, and making choices that are good for you.

Unrealistic Standards – Being so afraid of getting hurt again that you've listed every possible attribute of humankind on your list for Mr. Perfection. Given he doesn't exist, the list becomes a guarded barrier to finding the man you seek, instead of a list of what you want and need.

Walk on Water Attitude – You've decided you are beyond fantastic and dare any man to prove otherwise. This attitude is fearful arrogance, not confidence.

We Allow It – Part of the reason B.A.T.s exist is women tolerate ridiculous behavior from men, and use the excuse "They're men and that's just how they are."

What Does it Take to Keep You? – Choosing an attitude of what's needed for a man to deserve you, instead of being stuck in the attitude of what you have to do or become to get him.

What Do You Know About Him Process – Three steps to help you discover what's truly important to you, and create the standards for Mr. Right for You. The process starts with Mr. Perfect criteria, then narrows the list to your Must Have's and Nice to Have's, then identifies your Deal Breakers.

What Was I Thinking? – The realization that you do have standards, will use them this time, and refuse to settle. It's a moment to celebrate!

You'll Find Him When You Stop Looking – Fundamentally, this is about a change in your emotional state. Because you've worked on yourself, you shift from searching for him from a state of desperation combined with "sick and tired of being alone" - to feeling happy with yourself and your life, and being open to the possibilities. That's a much more attractive state of being and will interest a good man you would actually want in your life.

You're Still Here – Realizing that even after a heartbreak, you are still alive and kickin' and living your life.

CPSIA information can be obtained at www.ICGtesting.com
Printed in the USA
LVOW041921120912

298461LV00002B/1/P